Naturalist's Big Bend

Naturalist's Big Bend

An Introduction to the Trees and Shrubs,
Wildflowers, Cacti, Mammals, Birds, Reptiles
and Amphibians, Fish, and Insects

By Roland H. Wauer

 Texas A&M University Press   COLLEGE STATION AND LONDON

Library of Congress Cataloging in Publication Data

Wauer, Roland H.
    Naturalist's Big Bend.

    Bibliography: p.
    1. Zoology—Texas—Big Bend region. 2. Botany—
Texas—Big Bend region. 3. Big Bend National Park.
I. Title.
QL207.W38 1979   574.9764'932   78-21776
ISBN 0-89096-069-0
ISBN 0-89096-070-4 pbk.

Manufactured in the United States of America
REVISED EDITION

Contents

Illustrations

Preface

THIS edition of *Naturalist's Big Bend* is an updated version of the 1973 book, intended to provide the reader with a smorgasbord of facts about the natural resources of Big Bend National Park and vicinity. It is not intended to be a complete almanac of natural science, but rather a biological introduction to one of America's truly outstanding natural systems.

The book is composed of eleven chapters that lead from a geographical introduction into the various disciplines of flora and fauna and finally conclude with a bibliography. This last section serves as a valuable tool for the more serious disciple of the Big Bend Country, providing the investigator with a comprehensive set of references on the area.

It is impossible to complete a project of this kind without the aid of others. The initial manuscript and publication were supported by many neighbors and friends during my six-year residency in Big Bend National Park. I wish to thank Carolyn Borden for the fine pen sketches of plants; Jim Tucker for reading the manuscript; John Baccus, Lyman Benson, André Blanchard, Roger Conant, Cliff Crawford, Clark Hubbs, Roy Kendall, Lloyd Pratt, Jim Scudday, Herbert Stahnke, Arnold Van Pelt, and Barton Warnock for identification of specimens; Isabelle Conant, Mark R. Hopkins, Richard D. Porter, and the National Park Service for supplying photographs; and George and Mabel Burdick, Sammy Burdick, Joe Carithers, Clifford Casey, Cecil Garrett, Ross Maxwell, and Noberto Ortega for moral support.

The present edition proved to be more of a task than anticipated, and it would not have been completed without the support of Peter Scott, who helped to revise the bibliography, and Frank Deckert, Chief Naturalist, Big Bend National Park.

Naturalist's Big Bend

1. Within the Big Bend

HALFWAY between El Paso and Laredo, Texas, the Rio Grande forms a great southward arc into the Mexican states of Chihuahua and Coahuila. Known south of the border as the Rio Bravo del Norte, the Rio Grande is only a shadow of its former self. Most of the water of this once-proud river is used for agriculture long before it reaches El Paso, where it is often only a trickle.

It is the Rio Conchos, flowing out of the highlands of Mexico's Sierra Madre Occidental, that supplies most of the water that passes through the Big Bend Country. The Rio Conchos is controlled in Mexico by the newly created Granero Dam. Released water follows the irrigated valleys of eastern Chihuahua before pouring into the Rio Grande at Presidio, Texas. Tamayo (West 1964) reported that the Rio Conchos supplies 18 percent of the Rio Grande's total flow. The Rio Grande (Atlantic drainage) covers an area of approximately 765,000 square miles, of which 51 percent is within Mexican territory. Almost one-half of the Rio Grande's annual discharge is derived from Mexican tributaries.

Some geologists believe that the Rio Conchos, not the Rio Grande, was the ancestral river instrumental in the formation of the great canyons and adjacent landscape of the Big Bend Country (Charles B. Hunt, personal communication). It was the Rio Conchos that cut across the uplifting limestone sediments to carve Santa Elena, Mariscal, and Boquillas canyons. Although the structural patterns were formed during the Mesozoic (approximately 200 million years ago), events during the Tertiary (75 to 100 million years ago) built the present physical characteristics through emergence, folding and faulting, and erosion. Little has been added to the configuration of the landscape since.

Physiographically, the Big Bend lies within the southern portion of the Basin and Range Province. The northern edge of the Mexican Plateau forms its southeastern border. Geologists note that the south-

The Mesa de Anguila forms an impressive barrier along the western edge of Big Bend National Park. Here are the deep cut of Santa Elena Canyon and the confluence of the Rio Grande and Terlingua Creek. Photo by Wauer.

ward bend of the Rio Grande occurs at the place where the Front Range of the Rocky Mountains, diminished in height, forms the connecting link between the mighty ranges of New Mexico and Colorado and the majestic Sierra Madre of Mexico. The upstream course of the river is parallel to the direction of the Rocky Mountains folding for 100 miles. Downstream, it flows for some 75 miles in a direction parallel to the older mountains of the eastern United States, the Marathon-Ouchita Mountains. The Texas Big Bend is the only region where the two great mountain trends of our country are said to cross one another.

Within this Big Bend is a terrain that has been used by astronauts to simulate the moonscape. Much of the lowlands is of a forbidding character, shunned during the summer by even the experienced desert traveler. Here and there stand massive upthrust and eroded pillars, peaks, and mesas, all contorted seemingly far beyond the normal for such igneous structures. Yet time heals even the wounds of the earth. The open flats feature a skimpy and polka-dotted association of cacti, ocotillo, and other thorny desert plants. The drainages that carry a little more life-giving moisture support a slightly more luxuriant flora. And as elevation increases, this vegetation gives way to that produced by more than ten inches of annual rainfall, considered normal for deserts. Most of the mountains have woodlands not too dissimilar from other southwestern highlands; and in a few isolated canyons high enough to retain relatively moist conditions all summer long, forest-type vegetation exists.

The most striking example of all this diversity is preserved as a national park. A total of 708,221 acres of desert and mountain landscape was established as Big Bend National Park on June 8, 1944. Elevation extremes are 1,800 feet along the river near Stillwell Crossing and 7,835 feet at the summit of Emory Peak. The park's latitude is about the same as that of the mouth of the Mississippi River.

It is next to impossible to point out even a few of the significant biological aspects of such an area. Big Bend is one of the greatest of America's national parks, a biological paradise that more and more scientists and laymen are discovering.

Big Bend's lowlands can be regarded as the best example of the Chihuahuan Desert. Since 1944 this area has been free of cattle, sheep, and goats, animals that earlier had been a serious threat to the native vegetation. Over 40,000 head of stock were removed from park lands just before the park was established. In Mexico, the Chihuahuan Desert and grasslands provide that country's best grazing. Big Bend National Park stands alone as the only large acreage of Chihuahuan Desert and grasslands where the natural effects of geography and climate alone are allowed to shape the land and its animals and plants.

Near the center of the park, the Chisos Mountains form an igneous mass of intrusives and extrusives rising out of the Chihuahuan lowlands. The Chisos are the southernmost mountains within the United States and may be considered to be the only contiguous range within a national park. Like an island, the Chisos are biologically isolated, surrounded by an "ocean" of Chihuahuan Desert. Today's artificial world has left few places where native wildlife survives virtually uninhibited by man's interference, as it does in Big Bend National Park.

The Texas Big Bend Country has experienced a history of natural change. Philip V. Wells (1966) found that he could identify and date an

The South Rim, 7,200 feet elevation, is located at the southern edge of the Chisos Mountains. Photo by Wauer.

area's past and present vegetation through the study of wood rat deposits found in caves and other dry places. Excavations of numerous *Neotoma* "middens" from the foothills of the Chisos Mountains and Burro Mesa, down into the surrounding lowlands, resulted in some startling discoveries. Wells found foliage of a pinyon that no longer exists in the area. Radiocarbon dating revealed that 15,000 to 20,000 years ago the vegetation of the desert valleys, such as that along Marvillas and Tornillo creeks, was similar to that of the Chisos Basin today.

Wells theorized that conditions during the Pleistocene were considerably more moist than today. Approximately 10,000 years ago the climate began to change from one of relatively high precipitation to one of low rainfall. One can therefore assume that the Chihuahuan Desert of West Texas is rather recent (in geologic time), having developed only during the last 10,000 years.

There is little evidence of the faunal changes that took place during the drying period. Earlier animal life has been studied by a number of paleontologists, whose discoveries are summarized by John Wilson (Maxwell et al. 1967). More recently, the Sierra del Carmen Whitetail

Terlingua Creek and the cliffs of the Mesa de Anguila near Santa Elena Canyon.

The Rio Grande at Rio Grande Village with the Chisos Mountains in the background.

Boquillas, Mexico, below the limestone cliffs of the Sierra del Carmens.

Ernst Tinaja and the Deadhorse Mountains.

Deer offer an interesting example of change caused by alterations in the climate. Today, this whitetail is found only in the Chisos Mountains and in Mexico's Sierra del Carmens. During the Pleistocene, before the establishment of the Chihuahuan Desert, however, the two populations were apparently contiguous. As periods of aridity began to occur and to become more prolonged, the flora underwent extensive change. The tree line began to shrink into the mountains as the drying lowlands became a desert. More mobile animals were able to find more comfortable conditions. The Whitetail found suitable food, protection, and other necessities in the mountains. Although it may have taken hundreds of years, two separate populations of deer came into existence—that of the Chisos and that of Mexico's Sierra del Carmens. Today each still exists on its biological island, surrounded by an inhospitable "ocean" of Chihuahuan Desert. And sometime during the last few thousand years, the Mule Deer arrived in the lowlands and learned to survive in the desert that surrounds our Chisos island.

The Sierra del Carmens form the eastern boundary of the park. Here the Rio Grande meanders through the desert lowlands past the Mexican village of Boquillas into Boquillas Canyon. Photo by Wauer.

2. Man—A User of the Land

THE little that is known about man within the Big Bend Country before the arrival of the Europeans is based upon archaeological evidence accumulated over the years by a handful of workers. The West Texas Historical and Scientific Society of Alpine surveyed a number of archaeological sites, primarily in the northern part of the Big Bend, during the 1920's. M. R. Harrington (1928) excavated three rock shelters in Pine Canyon in 1928. Frank M. Setzler (1935) carried out excavations in the vicinity of Mule Ears Peaks in the early 1930's. And J. Charles Kelley, T. N. Campbell, and D. J. Lehmer (1940) reported on the association of archaeological materials with geological deposits in the Big Bend region of Texas.

Erik K. Reed (1936), a National Park Service archaeologist, examined 45 sites within the boundary of the proposed park in 1936, and Ruel L. Cook (1937) continued this study the following year. Although their reports were rescued, artifacts from their 277 sites were lost in a fire that destroyed one of the Civilian Conservations Corps buildings in the Chisos Basin.

During the summers of 1966 and 1967, Tom Campbell was contracted by the Park Service to survey the park's archaeological resources. Along with his assistants, Jim Corbin and Bill Field in 1966, and Mike Collins and John Eng in 1967, Campbell recorded 351 new sites. Campbell's 1970 report represented the first comprehensive analysis of the Big Bend's archaeology.

Earliest occupants have been dated back to about 9000 B.C.; Campbell found only casual evidence of these Paleo-Indians within the park area. However, he did find considerable evidence for the probability that at least two later distinct cultural groups, the peoples of the Archaic and Neo-American cultures, lived there before the coming of the Spanish influences, dating from about 6000 B.C.

These two groups apparently ranged throughout the entire Big Bend Country, although most of their remains have been found near water sources. It is assumed, therefore, that the climate and the food and water resources were essentially the same as they are today. These early inhabitants were hunting and food-gathering peoples who roamed from place to place with the seasons, occupying caves and rock shelters on an intermittent basis only.

The Archaic peoples hunted modern game animals using throwing sticks (called *atl-atls*) with dart points. They made extensive use of native plants for food and spent the greater portion of their time in the pursuit of food. The Neo-Americans had acquired the bow and arrow. Although this invention allowed them to obtain food more easily, they still were nomadic and moved with the seasons. It is likely that toward the latter part of this period there was some mixing of customs with the people to the west who farmed the rich floodplain of the Rio Grande.

These West Texas "cave dwellers" were still in existence when Cabeza de Vaca traveled through the area in 1535. Although de Vaca found agricultural practices common in the valley where Presidio and Ojinaga now exist, it is unlikely that much farming took place on the lands adjacent to the Rio Grande and its tributaries in the Big Bend National Park area.

The Spanish Influence

Spanish influences began with the penetration northward soon after the fall of the Aztec capital of Tenochtitlán in 1521. Within thirty years colonists and adventurers made contact with the desert Indian nation in Coahuila, Chihuahua, and southern Texas. With the Spanish drive north, the first information on the native Laguneros, Salineros, Tobosas, and Chisos began to be recorded. However, William B. Griffen (1969) believes that enough time had passed for some degree of acceptance of cultural items (such as the horse), population decline due to the spread of disease, and population shifting to have already taken place.

Indians of the Greater Bolson area—as the region from the Big Bend to Saltillo, Durango, and Parral, Mexico, was known—first encountered Spaniards who were either miners prospecting for silver and gold or Franciscans prospecting for souls. These Indians resented the Spanish encroachment upon their territories. The Spaniards' use of the Indians as slaves to work in the mines was an abuse that led to bloodshed and, eventually, to the decline of the desert Indians.

By the 1640's, the Tobosas, Salineros, Tepehuanes, and Chisos had fairly well-established raiding patterns against the Spaniards. When Jeronimo de Morata was "elected" to lead the entire nation against the Spanish in 1644, a peak effort was reached that continued, with fluctuations, for the next half a century. However, for a brief period in the early 1650's, the Spanish employed Saliñeros to fight against their old enemies, the Tobosas and the Chisos. Since the Chisos and Tobosas had long been bitter enemies themselves, the Chisos often joined the Saliñeros on raids against the Tobosas. And in 1654, a Chisos band joined Tobosas in raids upon Spanish mines (Griffen 1969).

Spanish policy toward the "frontier natives" was at first that of obtaining peace and imposing civilization by the sword. This approach was unsuccessful, and so a new practice of kind treatment and land purchase was adopted. The Spaniards, knowing that they could not live in constant strife with hostile Indians, selected the more peaceful

This aerial view was taken over Mariscal Canyon looking northward toward the Chisos Mountains. The side canyon that cuts across Mariscal Canyon is Smuggler's Crossing, a historic route over Mariscal Mountain into Mexico. Photo by Wauer.

method. The mission system was chosen to accomplish the goal of "civilizing" the desert Indians and, at the same time, to "bring the word of God to the heathen." Despite major setbacks, this system began to achieve the desired results.

Although no knowledgeable estimates have been offered of the numbers of native Indians within the Greater Bolson prior to the Spanish colonization of northern Mexico, an indication of the population was sent to the king of Spain by the "Oidor of the Royal Audiencia of Mexico" as late as 1678 (Carroll 1968, ch. 2, p. 7):

> Within the jurisdiction of the Kingdom of Nueva Vizcaya there are many distinct nations, some of which are very large. Those of the Tepeguanes, Taraumares, and Conchos alone in what has been explored, will total 300,000 families. . . . When the Indians at the last point to which the padres have gone are questioned as to whether there are more Indians further on and on either side, they reply that the multitude is innumerable in every direction. Solely on the Rio del Norte, which is the boundary of Nueva Vizcaya, there are so many nations that with all of their efforts the padres who are in that vicinity have not learned their names.

By the 1690's the appearance of the new Indian nations from the north—the Apaches, Janos, and others—contributed to more concerted efforts by the Spaniards to dispense with the raiding Indians. By 1693, five major defensive points were set up against the desert raiders at El Pasaje, El Gallo, Cerro Gordo, Parral, and Durango.

During this period the Saliñeros and Cabezas were almost totally exterminated (Griffen 1969), and the Tobosas became the undisputed leaders of the desert raiders. More and more Indian tribes began to make peace with the Spaniards. The "peaceful" Indians usually were deported to villages a considerable distance from their *rancherías*. About 350 Chisos were settled at San Francisco de Conchos. And in 1698, the Cocoymes, a Tobosa tribe, made peace and later settled at the abandoned mission of San Buenaventura de Atotonilco.

By the 1720's the original inhabitants of the Greater Bolson region were well on their way to extinction. The southern Coahuileño groups (the Saliñeros and Cabezas) and the Tobosas had just about vanished. The main groups that remained uncontrolled during the 1730's were the wild back-country dwellers from the northern part of the area adjacent to the Rio Grande, the northern Coahuilenos and the Chisos.

By the 1740's, however, Apaches became so dominant that they literally took over the entire region. Survivors of the original populations were either absorbed or exterminated. The last sixteen known Sisimbles, a tribe of the Chisos, were captured in 1748 and imprisoned in Durango.

Now it was the Apaches whom the Spaniards had to fight rather than the desert natives, and for the next fifty years it was the Apaches who controlled the Big Bend Country. The land that had served the earlier inhabitants as a place to camp and raise their crops continued to be used in the same way by the new landlords. Apaches, too, followed a hunting-gathering-raiding pattern. When the Spaniards provided them (unwillingly) with horses, their range was enlarged by hundreds of miles. They soon were as much at home in the mountains of the Big Bend as in New Mexico and Arizona. Apaches who resided within the Chisos Mountains, a name apparently derived from the early Indian nation of the same name, began to be known as the Chisos Apaches.

Apaches were not the only Indians who obtained the horse from the Spaniards. The Comanches, too, had horses and were able to expand their territory. They met opposition from the Apaches in the south and west, but by 1744 Comanches resided near Taos, New Mexico, and by 1790 the majority of the Apaches had withdrawn from Texas. Only a few of the smaller bands remained within the mountain fortresses, such as in the Davis and Chisos mountains.

The Spaniards had fought against the Indians for more than two centuries, but the Comanches became too strong for many of the settlements in northern Mexico. Raiding became so frequent at the beginning of the nineteenth century that the officials of New Spain were ready to concede the northern country to the Indians. For the first time the land of the Big Bend Country began to be abused, not by daily grazing and clearing of land but by regular forays of thousands of horses and warriors driving stock, slaves, and booty over a trail that cut directly through the Big Bend. Carlysle G. Raht (1919, pp. 63–64) wrote about the trail:

> Each year, in the light of the Mexican moon—for so they came to term the September full moon—the Comanche war trail swarmed with parties of these barbaric warriors, in troops of half-dozen to a hundred and more, including outlaws from many other tribes and even renegades from Mexico, who hurried forward to the carnival of bloodshed and rapine on the south side of the Rio Grande.

Along in November or December, following, the parties began to return. The great Comanche war trail then again presented an animated picture. A party here would be driving a herd of cattle; a party there, a troop of wild horses. In another band might be seen a small train of captives, herded and driven as any other beasts devoted to man's use. There might be great prairie fires started by a party of raiders to escape pursuit, while the party itself defected from the main trail.

But there was no way to cover or hide the Great Trail itself. It was worn deep by the hoofs of countless travelers, man and beast, and was whitened by the bones of many animals. It was a great chalk line on the map of West Texas, cutting through the heart of the Big Bend.

During the rest of the Mexican period in Trans-Pecos history the Comanches were at their height. In the early 1840's the Comanches' range was enormous, and the focal point of their activity was the Big Bend. In 1845, however, with the annexation of Texas by the United States, the federal government suddenly assumed the role of the defender. And with the discovery of gold in California in 1849, it became necessary to build a line of forts along the travel routes, thus dividing the Indian country in half.

With the eruption of the Civil War, however, these outposts were all but forgotten. Indian raids and other activities increased, and settlers moved to larger centers of habitation for their own protection. But at the end of the war when the military garrisons were reoccupied, families began to return to their homes. When the railroads arrived a few years later, the Indians' activity was gradually controlled.

The Ranching Years

Although a few families resided along the river where they raised goats and farmed small plots of land, most of the lower Big Bend Country had no settlers. The Estado Land and Cattle Company moved into this virgin country in 1885. Their 6,000 head of cattle increased to 30,000 head in six years (Gillette 1933). When the company disbanded in 1895, after several dry years, only about 15,000 head were rounded up from the G4 Ranch. However, the initial success of the Estado Land and Cattle Company had attracted other cattlemen. Dozens of smaller operators began to take advantage of the grasslands surrounding the Chisos Mountains.

One of the many ghost camps scattered throughout the Big Bend desertscape, Terlingua Abaja is located along the Old Maverick Road not far from Santa Elena Canyon. Photo by Wauer.

By the 1920's ranches encircled the Chisos Mountains. The majority of the ranching activity took place in the sotol-grasslands of the lower foothills. The higher parts of the mountains were fairly well protected by their inaccessibility. During the early decades of ranching the lowlands provided plenty of feed and stock rarely reached the higher canyons. As overgrazed lands developed in the lowlands, however, stock naturally moved upward. By the late 1920's the Chisos highlands began to be used heavily for grazing herds.

Although ranchers controlled the majority of the land within the Big Bend, most of the tillable lands along the Rio Grande and its tributaries were farmed. After the founding of the Terlingua Mining District at the turn of the century, a considerable portion of the flatlands was cultivated. A few of the farms remained in operation until the establishment of the national park.

Influences of the National Park Idea

In May, 1933, Big Bend State Park was established, with the Chisos Basin as its center. A Civil Conservation Corps (CCC) Camp was built in the Basin in May, 1934. A road was built up Green Gulch, and in 1940 cabins, improved trails, more roads, and visitor facilities were constructed. The CCC camp was finally abandoned in March, 1942.

On June 12, 1944, the congressional act that established a national park at the bottom of the Big Bend set aside 708,221 acres of desert and mountain terrain for future generations. Since the purposes of a national park include preserving an area in its natural state and attempting to restore the "natural processes" to their condition before the arrival of the first European, all uses of the land incompatible with these goals had to cease. Ranching, agriculture, mining, and other commercial enterprises within the park were terminated.

The Civilian Conservation Corps (CCC) Camp was located in the Chisos Basin about where the Basin Campground is today. National Park Service (NPS) photo.

The population within the area, just before establishment of the park, was approximately 155, equally divided between Mexicans and Anglos. Most of the Mexican families lived along the river. Typically, the wife worked a small garden plot, and the husband worked two or three months a year for one of the Anglo families. The rest of the year he grazed a few goats or was idle. This type of land use was casual but hard because the grazing animals had to subsist on desert land not really compatible for stock.

Most of the seventy-seven Anglos residing within the park were ranchers who lived on their land and had added miles of fences and other "improvements" such as wells, windmills, and earthen tanks for watering of livestock. The State of Texas purchased most of the privately owned ranches in 1942, and the ranchers were given free grazing privileges until the actual creation of the park in 1944. At the time the land was purchased, a total of 3,880 cattle, 9,000 sheep, 25,700 goats, and 310 horses were being grazed on the area (Prewitt 1947).

In 1944 and 1945, however, a total of 19,000 to 25,000 cattle, 6,000 to 8,000 sheep, 15,000 to 18,000 goats, and about 1,000 horses were removed from the area. The two years of free grazing privileges had been to the advantage of the ranchers, but the land had suffered. Too many stock had been placed on the soon-to-be-lost ranchlands. The tremendous increase in cattle was devastating to the land but beneficial to the ranchers' pocketbooks. There is every indication that ranching activities, particularly during the last two years, had a severe negative effect upon the native plants and animals in the accessible parts of the area.

Agriculture within the Big Bend was on a marginal or submarginal level prior to the establishment of the park. Of the four farms that had irrigated land, the largest was the La Harmonia Farm of 225 acres at Castolon. Farmers raised small gardens and a little cotton and wheat. The wheat was ground into flour and sold to the Mexicans. Most of the cotton was grazed rather than picked and ginned. Approximately 100 to 150 bales were produced on irrigated land in 1944. Some farmers had a little fruit, and most of the truck farming was of the garden type, producing only enough for the farmer's own use.

Farmers managed in the best of times, but in bad years they could not make a living. Farming reached a peak during World War I, but after the 1930's, the amount of wealth the land produced declined continually. The only sale of agricultural products involved small amounts sold in nearby towns after the items were transported there by wagon, horseback, or truck.

Mining was at a minimum when the park was established. Clifford B. Casey (1969*b*) reported that the Mariscal Mine produced and shipped 894 flasks of refined quicksilver from July, 1917 to May, 1919. With the decline of the quicksilver market after the war, the mine was closed and sold. Although it was reopened on occasion, it was never again a profitable venture.

Mariscal Mine, which lies on the northern point of Mariscal Mountain, contained a Scott furnace that was tended around the clock when the mine was in operation. "Mesquite wood was supplied by Mexican laborers who hauled it to the mine on burros, often as much as from fifty miles distance" (Casey 1968*a*, p.41). Woodcutting along the river for the Mariscal Mine, as well as considerable cutting in the Chisos Mountains for the Terlingua Mines, from 1900 through World War I, undoubtedly had ill effects upon the vegetation of these areas.

A hiker's view southwest from the western flank of the Chisos Mountains includes Goat Mountain (left center) and Castolon Peak (right background). Photo by Wauer.

In addition to these enterprises, three stores and a restaurant were in operation in the area when the park was established. All of these businesses, with the exception of the Castolon Store, whose sales averaged $3,000 per month, provided only a subsistence for their proprietors.

Guayule rubber and candelilla wax were also gathered and produced in the area. Rubber production had dropped to almost nothing by 1944, although the activity from 1916 to 1919 was significant. Candelilla business was and has continued to be an important enterprise along the Mexican border. An estimated 98 percent of that sold in the United States is now smuggled in from Mexico. Before the establishment of the park, this was an active enterprise indeed. Several major wax camps and factories existed at springs throughout the southern half of the park area. The gathering of the "weed," grazing of the pack animals, abuse and control of the spring sites, and related activities had quite undesirable influences on the native vegetation and wildlife.

The processing of native Candelilla at wax plants such as this one at Glenn Springs was an important enterprise during the early history of the park. NPS photo by Smithers.

The trapping of wildlife, predators as well as fur bearers, was another enterprise in the Big Bend. A government trapper resided in the area and was paid a salary based upon a bounty system and allowed to keep the pelts from fur bearers caught in season. His profit was substantial at first but marginal during the later years. Castolon's La Harmonia Company bought and sold pelts. Business "continued at a lively pace until about 1940, at which time the supply from the interior of Mexico dropped to the point that there was very little profit in the operation" (Casey 1967, p.77). In 1925, La Harmonia Company shipped fifty wolf hides to a dealer in the East. Although regular shipments were confined to raccoon, beaver, javelina, skunk, gray fox, and bobcat—animals that are still relatively common within the area—the sale of opossum, wolf, and "Mexican goat" (probably bighorn) pelts offers one clue to the extirpation of these animals from the Big Bend.

3. The Living Scene Today

IF you knew plants well enough you could identify your location anywhere on earth. Even if blindfolded and taken by air to some remote section of the United States, when your blindfold was removed, you could recognize your approximate location. As an example, where would you be if you found yourself amidst a woodland of Organ Pipe and Saguaro cacti? Easy? It is if you know the range of desert plants. You would be in southern Arizona, probably in or near the Ajo Mountains. Where would you be if your first view of the landscape revealed Joshua Trees, Saguaros, and Ocotillo? Another easy one? You would be in northern Arizona, not too far from Williams. Joshua Trees are indicators of the Mojave Desert just as Saguaros are indicators of the Sonoran Desert.

The point is that all of the world's great biomes, huge areas of similar plant types, possess key plant species. The Chihuahuan Desert is no exception. If you opened your eyes to see Lechuguillas and Blind Prickly Pears you would immediately know that you were located somewhere in the lowlands of the Chihuahuan Desert near the Rio Grande.

Each of the world's major vegetative zones contains smaller units that also feature characteristic plant species. These environments are called formations and are useful in classifying vegetative units within Big Bend National Park. The author (Wauer 1971) used five formations in describing the park's ecological zones:

River Floodplain–Arroyo Formation: 1,800 to 4,000 feet elevation
Shrub Desert Formation: 1,800 to 3,500 feet elevation
Sotol-Grassland Formation: 3,200 to 5,500 feet elevation
Woodland Formation: 3,700 to 7,800 feet elevation
Moist Chisos Woodland Formation: 5,000 to 7,200 feet elevation

River Floodplain–Arroyo Formation lies adjacent to the river and its lowland tributaries and consists of only a minute part of the park's total acreage. Plants of this formation usually grow in water-holding soils, are fast-growing, mostly broadleaf trees and shrubs, and often

Floodplain vegetation appears along the Rio Grande wherever open flats are regularly flooded by the river. This scene was taken from the Rio Grande Village Nature Trail, looking west toward the Chisos Mountains. Photo by Wauer.

The Big Bend desert lies below the wooded slopes of the Chisos Mountains between 3,500 elevation and the Rio Grande. NPS photo.

A belt of grasslands circles the Chisos Mountains between 3,500 and 6,500 feet elevation. This view of Green Gulch includes a Century Plant in bloom. NPS photo.

produce a dense, junglelike environment. Some of the most accessible units of floodplain are on the Rio Grande Village Nature Trail and just downriver from Santa Elena Canyon.

Shrub Desert Formation is the kind of area that most people think about when the desert is mentioned. It is an area characterized by less than ten inches of rainfall annually. The plants are widely spaced, relatively low growing, and many are succulents and semisucculents. Most have spines or seasonal leaves. Forty-nine percent of the park's total acreage is Shrub Desert.

Sotol-Grassland Formation occurs just above the desert, where precipitation is greater. The environment of widely spaced plants gives way to grasses and associated species. Fingers of grassland may extend far up into the mountain woodlands. Like the Shrub Desert, this is an extensive formation in the park and makes up about 49 percent of the total acreage. The formation is characterized by many grasses and little

Looking east toward the Chisos Mountains from the Maverick badlands.

Mule Ears from the Dodson Trail.

The Chisos Mountains from the Grapevine Hills. Notice Panther Junction in the upper left.

Sotol Vista looking west across the sotol-grasslands.

This aerial photograph of the Chisos Mountains was taken above Juniper Canyon looking west into the Chisos highlands. Notice the high point (Emory Peak) in about the center, and the flat, wooded slopes of the South Rim area to the left. Photo by Wauer.

open ground, and the majority of the plants are low growing; tall shrubs are more numerous here than in drier zones.

Woodland Formation occurs above the grasslands and extends to the top of the Chisos Mountains. Dominant plants of this zone are trees that may be divided into the broadleaf and coniferous types. Only 2 percent of the park's acreage is woodland.

Moist Chisos Woodland Formation occurs at only a few places in the high Chisos canyons. It consists of only 800 acres of "forest-edge" type vegetation within Boot and Pine canyons and along the northeastern slope below the East Rim.

4. Trees and Shrubs

TREES and shrubs usually are the most obvious plants within any given area and so are important indicators of plant zones. A rather distinct environment of relatively dense vegetation exists along the Rio Grande floodplain and at springs and other water areas up to the mountain woodlands. The **Lanceleaf Cottonwood** (*Populus acuminata*) is the largest tree of this environment. It is the park's only native cottonwood and once was much more abundant than it is today. There is now but one native grove left between Langtry to the east and Presidio to the west; about 150 trees occur below Castolon, along the Santa Elena Crossing Road (Mexico). A few native cottonwoods can also be found near Boquillas Crossing and just above Terlingua Abaja, and many have been planted in the campgrounds at Rio Grande Village and near Castolon.

Lanceleaf Cottonwoods were almost completely exterminated by early woodcutters for mines and buildings. The Spanish word for cottonwood is *alamo*, and Terlingua Creek was once called Alamo Creek because of the abundance of these trees along its banks. James B. Gillette (1933), foreman of the G4 Ranch from 1885 to 1891, described an 1885 scene at the confluence of Rough Run and Terlingua Creek as follows: "It may be interesting to know that at the time this ranch was established in 1885 the Terlingua was a bold running stream, studded with cottonwoods and was alive with beaver. At the mouth of Rough Run there was a fine grove of trees, under the shade of which I have seen at least one thousand head of cattle. Today (1933) there is probably not one tree standing on the Terlingua that was there in 1885"(pp.82–83).

None of the floodplain plants possess such an affinity for moist soils as do the **Common Reed** (*Phragmites communis*) and **Giant Reed** (*Arundo donax*). These plants are the tall "cane" found all up and down the river. Although Giant Reed is the taller of the two, both possess large, whitish flower heads that are borne at the top of the stalks.

Dugout Wells is one of the many isolated oases in the desert lowlands of the park. This area along the Panther Junction to Boquillas highway provides good shade and relaxing atmosphere for a short stop. Photo by Wauer.

Common Reed is native to the park, but Giant Reed has been naturalized in the United States, probably during the last fifty years. Both are used in Mexico for fencing and rooftops.

Other trees of mesic (wetter) soils include the willows. Four kinds have been found within the park. The **Southwestern Black Willow** (*Salix gooddingii*) is the largest and occurs along the floodplain and at springs at higher elevations. The **Black** (*S. nigra*), **Sandbar** (*S. interior*), and **Yew-leaf** (*S. taxifolia*) willows are fairly well restricted to the vicinity of the Rio Grande.

Here and there on the floodplain you may find a green-branched tree appropriately called **Texas Paloverde** or **Retama China** (*Cercidium texanum*). Although it is never abundant, good numbers of this yellow-flowering tree grow along the Santa Elena Crossing Road, as well as along the Floodplain Community Nature Trail a couple of miles below Santa Elena Canyon. This evergreen is only one of the many plants found in this environment that are members of the Legume (Pea) Family. Two common ones are **Screwbean** (*Prosopis pubescens*) (plate 1) and **Honey Mesquite** (*P. glandulosa*) (plate 1). The latter species is widespread throughout the park and can be found as high as 5,000 feet elevation. It is most numerous along arroyos near the river, where dozens of these tree-shrubs may produce thickets called *bosques*, after the Mexican word for forest or grove.

The Mexican name for Screwbean is *tornillo*, thus the name of the creek that drains the north and east side of the park. Once you have seen Screwbean you will not confuse it with the more common Honey Mesquite. Screwbean foliage is more lacy and the fruits are considerably different. Beans of Honey Mesquite have the shape of garden beans; they are green at first but tan when ripe. The fruits of Screwbean give the plant its name; they occur in clusters of tightly curled pods. The beans of both were used by Indians for flour. Fresh green beans of Honey Mesquite can be very sweet, and Mexican children suck them like candy.

Acacias are Legumes as well. Several kinds are found on the floodplain. The most beautiful of these, the **Black Brush** or **Chaparro Prieto** (*Acacia rigidula*), occurs only rarely in the park—in arroyos near the river along the eastern end of the River Road and to Glenn Springs. In early spring (February 20 to March 25) these sweet-smelling shrubs produce an abundance of bright yellow flowers that are some of the first blooms to attract hummingbirds. A little later, **Catclaw Acacia** or **Guajillo** (pronounced wa-HE-ah) (*A. berlandieri*) (plate 2) and **Huisache** (WE-satch) (*A. farnesiana*) take their turn to flower. Catclaw Acacia is a low-growing plant with decurved spines that suggest its commonly used name. The flowers of this species grow in cylindrical spikes, whereas those of Huisache are round and bright yellow. Huisache is the tree-Acacia that is quite common in and around Rio Grande Village Campground.

Common Buttonbush (*Cephalanthus occidentalis*) grows in moist places such as on the Rio Grande Village Nature Trail. Its round white flower heads seem to attract an abundance of butterflies. Nearby can usually be found woody grapevines that cling to the cliffs or to shrubs and trees.

In recent decades, a great portion of the southwestern floodplains and arroyos have been taken over by a tree that may form thickets dense enough to crowd out most of the other vegetation. This is an exotic called **Tamarisk** (also **Athel** and **Salt Cedar**) (*Tamarix* sps.), which was introduced into this country from North Africa for windbreaks and ornamentals in the Southwest. It is now the scourge of the floodplain. Only a few native animals are able to live among its salty foliage.

Tree Tobacco (*Nicotiana glauca*) (plate 1) is another little tree of the floodplain, although it also occurs at higher elevations. With long, tubular, yellow flowers that bloom in summer, fall, and early winter, it is a favorite of hummingbirds, particularly in late fall and winter, when most other vegetative food sources are gone.

On the drier parts of the floodplain and along arroyos, the **Seep-willow** and **Desert Willow** or **Mimbre** (*Chilopsis linearis*) (plate 2) may be common. Neither is a willow. The first is a sunflower and is abundant along the Rio Grande and in all of the park's washes; five kinds have been reported. The common species along the river and in lower arroyos is *Baccharis glutinosa* (plate 2), which may be eight to ten feet high; it has long, lance-shaped leaves and produces clusters of whitish flowers in late summer. Desert Willows grow to fifteen feet or more and have beautiful orchidlike flowers during spring and summer, and beanlike fruits that may be six to ten inches long in summer and fall.

Arroyo environments may extend far up into the Shrub Desert. Because of more mesic conditions, arroyos contain shrubs that may be found well up within the grasslands. Three of these are **Buckthorns**, **Squaw-bush** (*Condalia spathulata*) (plate 2), and **Javelina Bush** (*Condalia ericoides*) (plate 5). Squaw-bush, or **Bluewood** as it is sometimes called, is a spiny, bluish-green evergreen shrub that may be eight feet high. It produces purplish fruits in May, June, and July. Almost every bird in the vicinity will partake of these juicy berries. Javelina Bush has dark purple fruits as well, but they apparently are not as tasty as those of Squaw-bush. This plant is spiny and produces beautiful yellow flowers during March and April.

Guayacán (*Porlieria angustifolia*) (plate 2) is another shrub with fruits that are commonly eaten by wildlife. In spring, this evergreen produces large clusters of showy purple to violet flowers that develop into small heart-shaped fruits. When the pods ripen and dry, the skin peels off to expose two shiny seeds, ranging in color from red to orange. Guayacan is common along the Rio Grande Village Nature Trail and at the Old Ranch.

The Lowlands

Many of the park's most fascinating plants are those that have adapted to survive in the hot desert. Many species of cacti are discussed in chapter 6. The most abundant of Big Bend's desert plants is **Lechuguilla** (*Agave lecheguilla*) (plate 3), which can be found almost everywhere in the desert and ranges far up the mountains on slopes facing south that have little protection from the summer sun. If you walk into the lowlands you cannot go far without finding these sharp, succulent leaves that grow in a loose rosette. Like all Agaves, this plant must grow for many years before blooming. Finally, out of the center of the leaves rises a flowering stalk five to ten feet high. It blooms for a few weeks, from the bottom to the top, then dies. Dr. Barton Warnock, dean of Chihuahuan Desert botany, claims that a Lechuguilla requires fifteen to thirty-five years before it flowers. Indians made baskets and ropes from the fibrous leaves, and cortisone was extracted from the leaves during World War II.

False Agave (*Hechtia texensis*) (plate 3) looks very much like the plant described above and sometimes grows side by side with it on limestone cliffs along the river. **Hechtia**, as it is commonly called, is one of those unique plants that occurs nowhere except on limy cliffs and slopes in West Texas and adjacent Mexico. It is abundant where the road passes through the limestone cliffs about one mile west of Boquillas Canyon. Hechtia flowers are inconspicuous, on stalks that seldom rise more than two or three feet above the spiny, reddish-tinged leaves. This plant is a member of the Pineapple Family, while the look-alike Agaves are Amaryllis or daffodils.

Another plant common to limestone soils in the lower Big Bend is **Candelilla** or **Wax Plant** (*Euphorbia antisyphilitica*) (plate 3). For almost a hundred years this plant has been an important economic resource in northern Mexico. The thin, candlelike stems are pulled from the ground, along with the roots, bundled on burros, and taken to a crude processing plant. Since water is an important commodity in the production of wax, camps are almost always located on the river or at springs. Water is boiled in large metal vats before handfuls of the "weed" are thrown in. A little sulfuric acid added to the mixture renders the natural wax from the plant. The wax foams to the top of the boiling water, where it is skimmed off and placed in cooling tanks. The cooled wax, relatively lightweight and yellow-tan in color, is broken into small chunks and hauled by burro to buyers who further process it before selling it to makers of candles, commercial waxes and polishes, phonograph records, and chewing gum.

Candelilla wax production is regulated in Mexico by the Bank of Mexico. Thousands of pounds of wax are processed annually along the Rio Grande. When quotas are filled in Mexico, many wax makers then smuggle additional wax out of Mexico to buyers in the United States at Lajitas, La Linda, and Alpine. Although most of the Candelilla plants harvested come from Mexico, this plant is also picked in out-of-the-way places in the park, which, if done extensively, seriously disturbs the fragile ecology of the environment. Therefore, constant surveillance of the more than 708,000 acres of wilderness is necessary. Within the park, Candelilla is most common on the limestone hills near Rio Grande Village and on Mariscal Mountain and Mesa de Anguila. It has been planted in front of the post office at park headquarters, Panther Junction, so that visitors to the park can be sure of seeing it.

Leather Stem, Dragon's Blood, or **Sangre de Drago** (*Jatropha dioica*) (plate 3) is another unique plant species of south Texas. Seldom more than two feet in height, the leatherlike, reddish-brown stems produce leaves only after rainy periods. When the stem is injured, a whitish sap emerges that turns red when exposed to the air.

The most common shrub of the desert is **Creosote Bush** (*Larrea tridentata*) (plate 2). In fact, this yellow-flowering plant is one of the most common plants of all four of North America's deserts. It is often called **Greasewood** by mistake; Greasewood is a plant of higher elevations that looks considerably different. Creosote Bush is the abundant green-leaved shrub that occurs almost everywhere below 4,000 feet in Big Bend National Park. Its very small leaves are covered with a resinous material that restricts evaporation, one of this plant's adaptations for desert survival.

Tarbush or **Hojasé** (*Flourensia cernua*) (plate 2) appears with Creosote Bush throughout much of the Chihuahuan Desert. In the park, it is most abundant between Panther Junction and the Grapevine

Hills and west to the Christmas Mountains. Both plants have small green leaves and yellow flowers. The easiest way to distinguish them is by the color of the trunks: that of Creosote Bush is gray-brown and that of Tarbush is black. Once you have seen their general appearance you will have no trouble identifying them at some distance.

The gray-leaved shrub common along the roadways in the low desert is **Four-wing Saltbush** (*Altriplex canescens*). Particularly common along the River Road but may be found in disturbed areas up to 5,000 feet elevation, it is most easily identified in summer and fall when it produces conspicuous four-winged seeds.

Mormon-tea or *Ephedra* (plate 2) occurs throughout the desert and grasslands and resembles a loose bundle of light green sticks. It is particularly common along the River Road and near Dog Canyon. At least three kinds of these "joint-firs" have been identified in the park. The common name was derived from the fact that the plants were used to make tea by early travelers. The result is a delectable beverage if it is not brewed too strong. After drying pieces of the plant, put four or five broken joints in a tea holder and place it in freshly boiled water for ten to fifteen minutes. With the addition of a little sugar (some people use cinnamon), you have a very tasty native drink.

We cannot leave the discussion of desert plants without mentioning **Ocotillo** (*Fouquieria splendens*) (plate 3). Although not confined to the Chihuahuan Desert (it is also common throughout the Sonoran Desert), some of the largest Ocotillos are about fifteen miles below Panther Junction along the Rio Grande Village Road. This shrub is sometimes called **Coachwhip** because it looks like many buggy whips stuck into the ground. In a spring after a wet winter, the dead-looking stalks put out dark green leaves and a brilliant red cluster of flowers at the top of each stalk. When Ocotillos are in full bloom and the various colors of flowering cacti dot the landscape, the desert reaches its peak.

The Foothills

Several of the grassland plants are members of the Lily Family: **Yucca**, **Sotol**, and **Basketgrass** are a few. Four kinds of Yucca are found in the park. The most famous of these—**Spanish Dagger** or **Giant Dagger** (*Yucca carnerosana*) (plate 5)—occurs throughout the Dead Horse Mountains and is particularly abundant at Dagger Flat. This

One of Big Bend National Park's most impressive plants is the Giant Dagger Yucca that is abundant on Dagger Flat. Photo by Wauer.

large Yucca blooms early in spring, from late March through April, so most park visitors never find Dagger Flat in full bloom. And since the species blooms only every two or three years, following wet winters and springs, you may consider yourself fortunate if you are lucky enough to be in the area when hundreds of huge fifteen-to-twenty-foot daggers are sending their white plumes skyward.

The most numerous of the park's Yuccas is **Torrey Yucca** (*Y. torreyi*) (plate 5), which blooms during all but the coldest and driest times of the year, from the banks of the Rio Grande to about 5,500 feet in the Chisos Mountains. This is a relatively large-leaved plant that is easily distinguished from the two fine-leaved Yuccas: **Beaked Yucca** (*Y. rostrata*) and **Soap-tree Yucca** (*Y. elata*). Beaked Yucca is common throughout the Dead Horse Mountains, while the Soap-tree Yucca is present along the river and in deeper soils elsewhere in the park. The best way to tell these look-alike Yuccas apart is by examining a leaf; the edges of Soap-tree Yucca leaves are smooth and yellowish, while those of Beaked Yucca are slightly serrated and whitish.

A distinct "belt" of vegetation, sotol-grasslands, extends around the Chisos Mountains between 3,500 and 5,500 feet elevation. **Sotol** (*Dasylirion leiophyllum*) is easily recognized by its large cluster of serrated, narrow leaves that arise from near the ground. In the spring, whitish flowers appear on a tall, five-to-twelve-foot stalk. Sotol was used by Indians and early explorers in two ways. The "heart" of the plant was baked for food; all of the leaves were removed and the pineapple-sized center was placed on hot rocks left from a ground fire, covered with leaves and dirt, and allowed to bake overnight. The baked white heart is starchy but edible. Mexicans also boil chunks of the heart, let the juices ferment, and then distill the mixture to produce a drink of the same name. Although potent, it tastes like a mixture of hair oil and gasoline.

Bear-grass or **Mesa Sacahuista** (*Nolina erumpens*)(plate 5) looks very much like Sotol, but is really quite different. The whitish flowers, which bloom in summer, grow on a stalk that is seldom more than a foot or two above the leaves. The leaves are not toothed and are much finer than those of Sotol, actually drooping around the stalk. Indians used the leaves for basket making.

One of the most delicious fruits of the grasslands is that of a little tree called **Texas Persimmon** (*Diospyros texana*) (plate 5). It is difficult to find some of the large, deep purple fruits before they are harvested by the native animals; deer, coyote, gray fox, ringtail, and raccoon usually find them first. The fruits ripen anytime from July through November.

One of the earliest shrubs to bloom within the grasslands is **Desert Olive** (*Forestiera angustifolia*) (plate 5). I have found it blooming along the Dodson Trail in February and in Green Gulch in early March. Its deep purple flowers attract numerous insects, and a careful observer may also see an early hummingbird sampling the sweets from this member of the Olive Family.

Allthorn (*Koeberlinia spinosa*) (plate 3) also flowers early but has small and rather inconspicuous blooms. The branches of this plant are specialized for desert living in that they themselves are long spines. This shrub is usually less than five feet in height, but along the south side of the Chisos in the vicinity of Fresno Creek, are some that may be twelve feet high. These huge plants seem to offer excellent protection to desert mammals and birds that live among their sharp fortresses. The **Desert Hackberry** or **Granjeno** (*Celtis pallida*) is another shrub with many spiny branches. Like those of the Allthorn, the spines of the Granjeno protect the plant from browsers that might otherwise destroy it or severely limit its growth. Hackberry fruits are yellow to red and are edible.

Two kinds of Barberries occur in the park. **Agarito** (*Berberis trifoliolata*) (plate 5) is fairly common in the grasslands, while **Red Barberry** (*B. haematocarpa*) is a mountain plant, particularly common in Laguna Meadow. Both produce yellow flowers in spring (Agarito may bloom as early as February) and delicious little purple-red fruits in summer. Tiny spines on the leaves of these plants annoy whoever samples its delectable fruits.

More than two dozen Legumes occur in the Chisos Mountains. The catclaws of the grasslands usually are low-growing **Mimosas**. **Cat's-claw Mimosa** (*Mimosa biuncifera*) (plate 6) is most numerous in the foothills. It blooms in summer and produces delicate pinkish flower balls. Its leaflets are in pairs of five to twelve, while **Pink Mimosa** (*M. borealis*), another pink-flowering plant, has leaflets in pairs of three to eight. The two Acacias of this zone are **Mescat Acacia** (*Acacia constricta*) (plate 2) and **Catclaw** (*A. roemeriana*) (plate 6). Mescat Acacia is characterized by its long, white, straight spines, but the Catclaw has decurved spines and is similar to **Cat's Claw Acacia** of lower elevations. Mescat Acacia is another desert plant, easily identified in winter by its reddish appearance.

Feather Plume (*Dalea formosa*) (plate 6) is a low, rounded shrub that is particularly common along the roadways in lower Green Gulch and near park headquarters. This little Legume produces small, bright purple flowers that appear rather feathery when in bloom during spring and after summer and fall rainstorms.

Texas Mountain Laurel or **Mescal Bean** (*Sophora secundiflora*) (plate 6) is yet another attractive evergreen shrub of the Legume Family. This one bears showy purple flowers in spring and large peanutlike pods in summer and fall. The pods are so tough that it is almost impossible to break them. Inside are two to five red seeds that are poisonous to humans.

Mariola (*Parthenium incanum*) is a low-growing shrub with whitish branches and leaves. An indicator of overused land, it is abundant in some places, such as sites of old ranches from 2,500- to 5,500-feet elevation in the park. Mariola is very closely related to **Guayule** (y-OU-le) (*P. argentatum*), the **Mexican Rubberplant. Coldenia** (*Coldenia greggii*) is another of the gray shrubs found in this habitat. Its purple flowers grow in close, rounded heads. **Woolly Butterfly-bush** (*Buddleja marrubiifolia*) (plate 6) is a velvety shrub of the foothills often found in association with the above species. Flowers of this plant are borne in a head, too, but are cream to orange in color.

Watch, too, for a member of the Rose Family whose plumelike seeds give it the name **Apache-Plume** (*Fallugia paradoxa*) (plate 5). It is common in Green Gulch, below the upper water barrel, and in similar canyons throughout the mountains. The white flowers are roselike and appear throughout the summer. The feathery seeds persist until winter weather sets in.

Resin-bush (*Viguiera stenoloba*) (plate 6) is one of the most common yellow-flowering shrubs of the foothills and mountains during summer and fall. A much-branched plant that may be two to five feet high and bears many sunflowerlike blooms, it is common along the Lost Mine Trail and in drainages throughout the foothills. Resin-bush is closely related to **Zexmenia** (*Zexmenia brevifolia*) (plate 6), which occurs with it in the foothills. Zexmenia may be five feet in height but is more often two to three feet high, with five to eight rays to each of its rather small flowers. Resin-bush has about twelve rays per flower head.

Damianita (*Chrysactinia mexicana*) (plate 8) is a little shrub that bears numerous yellow flowers in summer and fall. The dark green foliage is strongly scented. If you pinch the leaves, the scent will remain on your fingers for quite a while. It is said that Indians brewed a tea from the foliage, which was used to induce abortions.

Of the many yellow-flowering shrubs of the grasslands, none is as showy as **Trumpet-flower** or **Esperanza** (*Tecoma stans*) (plate 7). Usually found on rocky hillsides, it produces numerous yellow trumpet-shaped flowers that may be two inches in length. The seedpods are long and beanlike, although it is a member of the Bignonia Family. Look for these plants along the Blue Creek Trail and similar places during late summer and fall. Also, a beautiful specimen is planted alongside park headquarters.

In many of the foothill arroyos grows a little tree that is seldom noticed until fall when its leaves turn yellow. This is the **Little** or **River Walnut** (*Juglans microcarpa*), common in the drainages along the roadway between park headquarters and Basin Junction. Like all walnuts, it has a hard seedpod. The nut is black and furrowed, seldom more then two-thirds of an inch wide.

Three Sumacs occur in the park. None is poisonous, although another member of this family, **Poison Ivy** (*Rhus toxicodendron*), can be found in a few of the protected and moist canyons along the base of the Chisos Mountains. **Evergreen Sumac** (*R. virens*) is common in the mountains and produces red berries in summer and fall. It has smooth green leaves that are one inch in length and half as wide. **Fragrant Sumac** (*R. aromatica*) occurs throughout the grasslands and mountains, and **Small-leaved Sumac** (*R. microphylla*) is a plant of the lower foothills and desert. Wildlife eat the fruits of all three, and Indians made a lemonadelike drink from the fruits as well.

Many of the grassland plants do not flower until the summer rainy season, although the greatest floral display is usually in spring. In dry years spring flowers may be few and far between. However, only rarely does the Big Bend Country not get its full share of precipitation during late summer. During this season the **Cenizos** bloom. There are three Cenizos, or **Silver-leafs**, in the park. Two are fairly common within the grasslands; *Leucophyllum frutescens* (plate 6) is a large plant with dark purple flowers, and *L. candidum* is a smaller shrub with deep violet flowers and oval leaves. The third is *L. minus*, a small plant with lavender-violet flowers and large leaves. Cenizos are often called **Pur-**

ple Sage, although they are not sages at all, but members of the Fig-wort Family.

Havard Agave (*Agave havardiana*) ranges from the grasslands well into the higher mountains. Early bloomers begin in April in the low-lands, and late bloomers have been found in the highlands through October. Like Lechuguilla, this plant dies the year that it flowers. It takes from twenty-five to fifty-five years before it finally sends up a ten- to twenty-foot stalk, branches appear along the upper half, and "plat-ters" of yellow blossoms cover the end of each branch. The flowers serve as nature's own smorgasbord; dozens of animals feast at these natural cafeterias.

Every year during the blooming season the National Park Service brings one of these plants to park headquarters, where the growth of the stalk is measured. During one twenty-four-hour period in May, 1968, a stalk grew sixteen inches. It takes many years before the plant is ready to bloom, but when once it starts, it "really goes to town." The long wait for flowers is why it is called "Century Plant."

The Mountains

As is expected, the largest plants occur in areas of greatest mois-ture. Trees are largest along the river and in the mountains. Most of the mountain plants are either conifers—pine, juniper, and cypress, or broadleafs—such as oak and maple.

Only two pines have been recorded in the Chisos Mountains. **Mexican Pinyon** (*Pinus cembroides*) is most abundant. It may be found almost everywhere above approximately 5,000 feet elevation in the Chisos Mountains and at localized areas in the Dead Horse Mountains. **Ponderosa Pine** (*P. ponderosa*) is restricted to two canyons. It is most numerous in Pine Canyon, where a fairly good stand of these tall pines occurs on the northern slope below Crown Mountain. This area has been established as the "Pine Canyon Natural Area" through the In-ternational Biological Program and is the southernmost stand of Pon-derosa Pines in the United States. This large conifer also can be found in Boot Canyon, where a few large trees occur along the south-facing slope and numerous young trees are growing among the pinyons and oaks within the lower drainage.

Three junipers occur in the park. The most famous of these is

Weeping or **Drooping Juniper** (*Juniperus flaccida*), which is found nowhere else in the United States but is common in woodland areas of Mexico and as far south as Central America. Its drooping foliage and stringy bark are easily identifiable characteristics. **Alligator Juniper** (*J. deppeana*) also has an easily recognizable characteristic: the bark looks like the gnarled back of an alligator. If the foliage does not droop and the bark does not have the appearance of an alligator, the tree is the third species, **Red-berry Juniper** (*J. pinchotii*). All are fairly common throughout the Chisos woodlands.

The last of the park's conifers is a magnificent tree that grows only in the Boot Canyon drainage, **Arizona Cypress** (*Cupressus arizonica*). This stately tree stands high above the rest of the vegetation and is most numerous in the narrow canyon above Boot Springs but also may be found in lower Boot Canyon and along the north ridge below the East Rim. This species may be a relict from colder and wetter times. It is not found elsewhere in Texas but is common in the highlands of the Fronteriza Mountains of northern Coahuila, about forty airline miles southeast. It also occurs in the mountains of southern New Mexico and Arizona.

Quaking Aspen (*Populus tremuloides*) is another possible relict species, found only on the high talus slope below the west and north sides of Emory Peak in the park. Park Ranger Eric Burr counted fewer than 225 of these trees in 1965. Recent examinations by the author indicate that they are doing well; there is no apparent decrease of these white-barked trees of the northlands.

One of the park's most beautiful broadleaf trees is a little red-barked plant called **Texas Madrone** or **Naked Indian** (*Arbutus texana*). It is most easily found near the upper water barrel in Green Gulch but is fairly common throughout the mountains. The bark is smooth and reddish in spring but peels off in summer, leaving a whitish underbark that eventually turns red. During summer, the peeling red bark gives the tree a strange appearance. This species makes an excellent ornamental and can be purchased at nurseries in nearby towns.

Also in Green Gulch, watch for the **Lead-tree** (*Leucaena retusa*) (plate 8) near the switchbacks on the east side of Panther Pass and above the lower water barrel. This little tree is similar to Huisache in the lowlands. Its round flower balls appear during summer after each rainstorm. Summer rains also bring flowers to a shrub that goes un-

Arizona Cypress is the largest of the park's plants. This species is common in Boot Canyon and on the upper slopes of Juniper Canyon. This scene is in Boot Canyon near Boot Springs. Photo by Wauer.

noticed during the rest of the year—the **Texas Kidney Wood** or **Vara Dulce** (*Eysenhardtia texana*) (plate 8), which has long, sweet-smelling white spikes of flowers during August and September. At first appearance, it is very similar to **White Brush** or **Troncoso** (*Aloysia gratissima*) that occurs in water-holding areas throughout the mountains. It is common near the Chisos Trailhead and Basin Amphitheatre.

Guauyul or **Palo Prieto** (*Vauquelinia angustifolia*) occurs sporadically in the Chisos Mountains (it is fairly common along the Window Trail) and in the highlands of the Dead Horse Mountains. This species is not found elsewhere in the United States, although it does occur in adjacent Mexico. It is a rather small evergreen tree with narrow, toothed leaves four to six inches long. A member of the Rose Family, it produces small and inconspicuous white flowers in spring and a woody capsule in summer and fall.

Two ashes occur in the mountains. **Gregg** or **Little-leaf Ash** (*Fraxinus greggii*) is a short, small-leaved tree that is common in drier canyons at middle elevations. The other, **Fragrant Ash** (*F. cuspidata*), is a larger tree that produces sweet-smelling flowers in early summer. Nearby can usually be found **Mountain Mahogany** (*Cercocarpus montanus*) (plate 8), with its white flowers and hairy fruits. This tall shrub is a member of the Rose Family and is a favorite browse plant for deer.

Netleaf Hackberry (*Celtis reticulata*) is common in the mountain canyons. Its leaves are ashlike but rough and strongly veined. The reddish-black fruits are a favorite food of birds. The low-growing shrub often associated with the later species is **Silk-tassel** (*Garrya wrightii*). Its leaves are evergreen and rather leathery, and its purple fruits are eaten by many kinds of wildlife.

Texas Buckeye or **Monilla** (*Ungnadia speciosa*) occurs in the cooler canyons within the lower elevations. In spring it is one of the first of the flowering trees to bloom, with delicate bright pink blossoms. In summer it produces large, three-lobed pods that contain dark brown poisonous berries.

There are two mints in the Chisos highlands that bear showy red flowers in summer and fall. **Cedar Sage** (*Salvia roemeriana*) is rare, but **Mountain Sage** (*S. regla*) (plate 8) is fairly common. The brilliant red flowers of these shrubs are more attractive to hummingbirds than are Century Plants, which may also be in flower at this late date. Mountain Sage is endemic to the Chisos Mountains.

In the higher canyons of the Chisos Mountains is **Sugar Maple** or **Mountain Maple** (*Acer grandidentatum*). It seems out of place in these desert mountains, for this is the same maple that produces the grandiose fall color displays in the Rockies and Sierras. Fall color arrives late in the Chisos; early November is usually the best time of the year to enjoy the changing colors in the Big Bend.

Oaks are numerous within the mountains, and their leaves often add bright colors to the fall display. As many as seventeen varieties of oaks have been identified in the park, but C. H. Muller (1951) recognizes only nine species; the rest are hybrids or combinations of two species. Oaks are well known for this characteristic, which sometimes makes their identification extremely difficult.

Three of the nine species are rather widespread in the Chisos: **Gray Oak** (*Quercus grisea*), **Emory Oak** (*Q. emoryi*), and **Grave's Oak** (*Q. gravesii*). The first is common and is most accessible along the roadway and on hillsides in Green Gulch. It is a low-growing tree with small gray-green leaves. Emory Oak prefers drainages at higher elevations but can also be found in Green Gulch just above the upper water barrel. Its leaves are lance-shaped, slightly spiny, dark green on top, and partly evergreen. The tree is named in honor of William E. Emory, who conducted a survey of the United States–Mexican border in 1857. Both Gray and Emory oaks have about the same range in the United States, from West Texas west to southern Arizona and south into Mexico. The last of the three common oaks is Grave's Oak, which is restricted to the mountains only in West Texas and northern Coahuila, Mexico. This is a deciduous red oak that also prefers canyons. Its leaves are two to four inches long, have deep rounded lobes, and are shiny dark green.

Two of the remaining oaks are considered shrub oaks because they are low-growing plants that form chaparral zones on mountain slopes and in swells. **Coahuila Scrub Oak** (*Q. intricata*) is known in the United States only in the Eagle and Chisos mountains, but it is a characteristic species in the Coahuilan chaparral. A large area along the north side of Laguna Meadow supports the species, and it also occurs along the upper section of the Lost Mine Trail. The other chaparral plant is **Vasey Oak** (*Q. pungens* var. *vaseyana*), which prefers limestone soils. This plant is common in the higher slopes of the Dead Horse Mountains but has not been found in the Chisos.

The remaining four oaks are localized. **Gambel Oak** (*Q. Gambelii*) occurs on the upper slopes of Casa Grande. This is the common oak of the southern Rocky Mountains, but its range also extends to West Texas and south into northern Mexico. **Chinkapin Oak** (*Q. muhlenbergii*) has been recorded in Pulliam Canyon in the park but is a common oak of the eastern uplands of the United States. One of the rarest oaks is the **Chisos Oak** (*Q. graciliformis*), which is endemic to the Chisos Mountains. This graceful little tree requires a high water table and is restricted to a few mountain canyons such as Blue Creek. The leaves are three to four inches in length, thin and leathery, and partly evergreen. The last of the Chisos oaks is another endemic that occurs only in upper Boot Canyon, the **Lateleaf Oak** (*Q. tardifolia*). This species forms a small erect tree with leaves that are somewhat spiny, two to two and a half inches long and one to two and a quarter inches wide, and dull bluish-green in color.

5. Wildflowers

THE majority of the more than 1,000 kinds of plants that have been reported for the park are wildflowers. Their habitat ranges from the riverbank to the top of the Chisos Mountains; at all times of the year at least a few species can be found in flower somewhere in the park.

The floodplain forms the lowest and warmest portions of the park. Trees and shrubs make up the bulk of the plant life, and wildflowers usually are at a minimum. **Texas Virgin's Bower** or **Old Man's Beard** (*Clematis drummondii*) (plate 1) and **Morning Glory** (*Ipomoea lindheimeri*) occur along the floodplain, growing upon their woody neighbors. The lovely blue-lavender flowers of Morning Glory brighten the floral picture during summer, and Virgin's Bower flowers appear in summer and fall. Male and female flowers are produced on different plants. Males are small, approximately one-half inch in length, but the females bear numerous long-styled pistils. The female fruiting heads are even more conspicuous, with long, slender, silky plumes that may be four inches long.

In places where the soil forms moist depressions, **Mexican Devil-weed** (*Aster spinosus*) (plate 1) and **Globe-mallow** (*Sphaeralcea angustifolia*) (plate 1) often dominate the environment. The cup-shaped, orange to whitish flowers of Globe-mallow appear in spring; but the tiny, white, daisylike blooms of Devil-weed do not appear until summer and fall. This species forms rather dense, low thickets along the Rio Grande Village Nature Trail, a good place to find all of the plants of this zone. Watch, too, for the little purple-flowered **Broomrape** (*Orobanche ludoviciana*) that occurs along the trail. Although inconspicuous at first, this is a beautiful flower when in full bloom.

Cowpen Daisy (*Verbesina encelioides*) (plate 1) is a common flowering plant of the open areas on the floodplain. Its yellow rays may be so numerous in places that much of the shoreline has a golden hue. There, too, can usually be found **Silver-leaf Nightshade** or **Trompillo** (*Solanum elaeagnifolium*) (plate 1), a purple-flowering species of disturbed areas. It also occurs near buildings and along roadsides to about 4,500 feet elevation. Mexicans use the round, yellowish fruits of this species to curdle milk for cheese.

The tiny, low-growing purple flower is **Purple Ground Cherry** (*Physalis lobata*), and the larger purple flowers with yellow centers are **Tahoka Daisy** (*Machaeranthera tanacetifolia*), which blooms into the foothills later in summer. The bushy, white-flowering Mustard is **Pepperwort** (*Lepidium montanum*), whose name was derived from its fruits and leaves, which are peppery to the taste.

Desert Baileya (*Baileya multiradiata*) (plate 4), the "desert sunflower," may be locally abundant as well. It blooms to elevations of about 4,500 feet during spring, summer, and fall, moving upward with the seasons. The little, rounded, gray-green plant, with minute yellow flowers, is **Espanta Vaqueros** (*Tidestromia lanuginosa*).

Look along the water's edge for **Bluebells** (*Eustoma grandiflorum*) (plate 1). This beautiful five-petaled flower may be pink to deep purple in color and blooms from late summer until winter weather sets in. It is common around the ponds adjacent to Rio Grande Village Campground.

The Lowlands

Open floodplain makes up about half of the southern boundary of the park. The other half consists of limestone cliffs that reach to the water's edge. Few plants grow upon the cliffs. One of these, however, **Rock-nettle** (*Eucnide bartonioides*), possesses beautiful, large yellow flowers that cover its dark green leaves (plate 3). Blooming from November through May, it is common along the rocky cliffs near the river and in the lower mountain canyons. Look for it at Hot Springs and near the tunnel above Rio Grande Village.

The rocky banks near the river seldom produce many flowers, but there are exceptions. **Umbrella-wort** or **Trailing Allionia** (*Allionia incarnata*) (plate 4) is a many-branched, creeping plant that may form extensive mats of light green branches and windmill-shaped, purple flowers that dot the rocky banks. In fall, **Spiderling** (*Boerhaavia linearifolia*) may be common in similar places in the lowlands. The very small, purple to magenta flowers of this long-stemmed perennial seem to stand apart from the rest of the plant. This late bloomer is particularly common along the roadside between Castolon and Santa Elena Canyon.

The desert in bloom can be an unforgettable sight. When late fall and winter precipitation has been normal, Big Bend's desertscape is a blaze of color.

One of the earliest flowers to put in its appearance is the **Chisos Bluebonnet** (*Lupinus havardii*) (plate 4). This is the West Texas Lupine and is a different species than the famous Texas Bluebonnet, the state flower, that is resident of the eastern half of the state.

Desert Verbena (*Verbena wrightii*) (plate 4) is another species that blooms all year around, on the desert in winter and spring and in the mountains the rest of the year. Its fragrant flowers are locally called Sweet William. The little purple-flowering Nama of open washes and gravelly flats is **Havard Nama** (*Nama havardii*). This is a little perennial with tiny hairs on its petals and strongly scented leaves. Another Waterleaf sometimes found in this association is **Phacelia** (*Phacelia coerulea*). This purple-flowering plant has deeply lobed basal leaves. **Gyp Phacelia** (*Phacelia integrifolia*) (plate 4) occurs on open flats in spring and in foothill arroyos in summer. Its basal leaves are heavily dissected. A walk over gravelly flats in spring may reveal the delicate, pinkish-violet flowers of **Edwards' Nicollet** (*Nicolletia edwardsii*), whose narrow green leaves produce a strong spicy scent when pinched.

Chisos Prickly Poppy (*Argemone chisosensis*) (plate 3) is one of the park's lowland specialties, although it also blooms in summer to 6,000 feet in the Chisos Mountains. This large poppy is easy to identify because of its typical poppy flowers, white to pink in color, and prickly stems and leaves. Sap in the stems and leaves is yellow.

Mesa Greggii (*Nerisyrenia camporum*) (plate 4) is another of the park's year-round bloomers. It can be the most common flowering plant of the desert in February and early March. Its white flowers turn pinkish with age. Basal stems are usually quite woody. This shaggy plant is a member of the Mustard Family. So is **Gregg Keelpod** (*Synthlipsis greggii*), a white- to rose-flowering herb, often present on open flats to 3,000 feet elevation. Watch, too, for a dainty little prostrate plant with tiny, white-margined leaves, **White-margined Sandmat** (*Euphorbia albomarginata*).

Desert Tobacco (*Nicotiana trigonophylla*) also produces white flowers during spring and summer. A member of the Potato Family, this one- to three-foot-tall plant was used by Indians for tobacco. The leaves were dried and ground into a tobacco that was smoked in homemade bone pipes. Desert Tobacco is a plant of rocky places, which can be found in the foothills as well as within the major canyons of the Rio Grande.

Look along road shoulders for **New Mexico Dalea** (*Dalea neomexicana*) (plate 7). This little Legume may be locally common during spring and after the summer rains. Here, too, sometimes can be found **Arizona Euphorbia** (*Euphorbia arizonica*) and **Woolly-flowered Spurge** (*E. eriantha*). The latter species is a narrow-leaved plant that bears flower-cups with whitish down.

There probably are more yellow flowers in Big Bend's desert bouquets than any other color. Some of the early bloomers include Desert Baileya, **Caliche Bahia** (*Bahia absinthifolia*), and **Parralena** (*Dyssodia pentachaeta*) (plate 4). All three are sunflowers. Bahia and Parralena may occur in numbers on desert flats in spring and after summer rains. The easiest way to distinguish between the two is to pinch them; Parralena is strongly scented because of minute glands on the bracts.

Fendler's Bladder-pod (*Lesquerella fendleri*) may also be common in the lowlands but seems to prefer the gravelly soils. Its fruits are small, round pods. And in summer, usually after the summer rains begin, a little yellow, low-growing plant called **Limincillo** (*Pectis angustifolia*) (plate 4) may be abundant. If you squeeze part of this plant you will readily understand why it is named for a lemon. Its odor can be almost overpowering.

Watch for a strange plant that looks more like a pile of yellowish spaghetti than a living plant. This is **Pretty Dodder** (*Cuscuta indecora*), a leafless parasite that is a member of the Morning Glory Family. It is a low-growing plant that lives on other plants. Dodder seeds germinate in the ground, the long stems twine themselves around a host plant, and suckers actually enter the host and absorb food.

The desert is often filled with a multitude of blooms after the summer rains begin. In fact, many springtime flowers bloom again. They are joined by other species that usually wait for the second blooming season. **Mexican Poppy** (*Kallstroemia grandiflora*) (plate 7) and **Berlandier Flax** (*Linum rigidum*) are two of the late bloomers that add a good deal of color to the summertime terrain. Both produce reddish to orange flowers that contrast greatly with the browns and light greens of the desert background. Mexican Poppy is a member of the Caltrop Family and is not a poppy at all. Its five petals may be two inches across. Berlandier Flax is a smaller plant with petals that are seldom more than half an inch across.

The Foothills

Grasslands are surprisingly extensive within nondisturbed areas of the Chihuahuan Desert. Grasses make up the major part of the environment, and as many as twenty to twenty-five species can be identified within a few hundred yards in many places. **Fluffgrass** (*Erioneuron pulchellum*) forms tiny clumps along roadsides and on open flats from the open, dry floodplain to about 5,000 feet elevation. **Tobosa** (*Hilaria mutica*) can be found in deeper soils and in protected swells between the floodplains and the lower foothills. The common foothill grass, **Chino Grama** or **Gyp Grama** (*Bouteloua breviseta*), is widely dispersed on all of the foothills surrounding the mountains. This is the dominant grass cover on the hills behind Dugout, north of Panther Junction, and on Burro Mesa.

By late February, flowers may begin to appear in the foothills—not too many at first, but as the season progresses their numbers increase. Several of the foothill species are the same as those blooming earlier in the desert. White flowers of Mesa Greggii blend well with yellow Fendler's Bladder-pod and purple Desert Verbena.

Red flowers seem to show up best among the grasses. **Braceted paintbrush** (*Castilleja latebracteata*) (plate 7) adds considerable color to the landscape, flowering from spring through fall. **Havard Penstemon** (*Penstemon havardii*) (plate 7) may be common along arroyos (it flowers along the east side of park headquarters throughout the spring months) where it sends up its tall stems that are lined with bright red blooms. The lavender-flowered penstemon found along the roadsides in Green Gulch is **Fendler's Penstemon** (*P. fendleri*).

Rouge-plant (*Rivina humilis*) prefers shady areas in canyons. Its inconspicuous white flowers are not good prophets for the bright red berries that are produced in fall. And during wet summers you may find **Arroyo Twine-vine** (*Sarcostemma cynanchoides*) and **Scarlet Morning Glory** (*Quamoclit coccinea*). Both are twining plants usually found growing on low shrubs. The latter species is one of the park's most beautiful flowering plants. Arroyo Twine-vine, one of the Milkweed Family, has elongated, heart-shaped leaves and clusters of pink and white flowers. **Bush Anisacantha** (*Anisacanthus insignis*) (plate 7) is another twining plant that receives its support from more woody plants. This can be a fairly common flower in summer and fall. Its orange to reddish flowers are two to three inches long and split into three parts on the upper half of the corolla.

Watch along the roadsides in Green Gulch for clumps of greenish to maroon flowers. This tall plant is **Antelope-horn** (*Asclepias asperula*) (plate 6), a Milkweed that blooms during April and May. Its name is derived from the pods, which split on one side to look like horns. The many brown seeds inside have silky hairs attached to one end.

Of the many white flowers within the grasslands, one of the most interesting is **White Milkwort** (*Polygala alba*), locally common along roadsides. Its delicate spikes of flowers appear during spring and summer, particularly after rainy periods. **Plains Fleabane** (*Erigeron modestus*) can also be found along roadsides, usually in the protection of grasses or other plants. This is a dainty little daisy with many white rays and a yellow center. **Plains Black-foot** (*Melampodium leucanthum*) (plate 7), a low, rounded herb that has fewer rays, with larger and more numerous flowers than Fleabane, occurs there, too. It is often the most common white flower found in the foothills. As the season progresses Plains Black-foot flowers at higher elevations where it may also be common. In the Dead Horse Mountains, **Zinnia** (*Zinnia acerosa*) seems to replace Black-foot of the Chisos Mountains.

Rock-trumpet or **Flor de San Juan** (*Macrosiphonia macrosiphon*) (plate 9) blooms in the foothills in spring and in the higher mountains in summer. Its long corolla, somewhat twisted like a pinwheel, may be four inches in length and is an excellent identifying characteristic of this species. **Varied-leaf Bean** (*Phaseolus heterophyllus*) and **Vetch** (*Vicia exigua*) also occur in this association. Both of these Peas may be common after the summer rains, although Vetch also blooms during spring.

Purple flowers of the foothills are well represented by **Hillside Vervain** or **New Mexico Verbena** (*Verbena neomexicana*) (plate 4). This neat little herb has an erect stem and delicate flowers that bloom from March, in the lowlands, throughout November, in the higher mountains. And a search along the slopes will usually reveal the bright blue flowers of **Widow's Tears** or **Day-flower** (*Commelina erecta*) (plate 7). This delicate flower has two large petals and a small one partially enclosed by the uppermost leaf.

Germander (*Teucrium cubense*) and **Common Horehound** (*Marrubium vulgare*) (plate 9) are excellent indicators of disturbed soils. Both of these plants are members of the Mint Family. They can be readily identified by the mint smell from a pinch of a leaf.

There are numerous yellow flowers in the foothills. **Senna** (*Cassia lindheimeriana*) occurs on rocky slopes; it is fairly common in summer along the Blue Creek Ranch Trail. Senna is a member of the Pea Family; the species of the lowlands is **Two-leaved Senna** (*Cassia durangensis*). **Indian Rush-pea** (*Hoffmanseggia glauca*) is another Pea of the foothills, although it also occurs along roadsides at lower elevations. This is a small, delicate plant that at first glance looks like a little *Astragalus*.

Showy Menodora (*Menodora longiflora*) and **Puccoon** or **Gromwell** (*Lithospermum incisum*) flowers are similar in appearance. Both have yellow tubular corollas, but the leaves of Puccoon are long and succulent while those of Showy Mendora are small and narrow. Indians made a purplish dye from the outer layer of the roots.

Woolly Paper-flower (*Psilostrophe tagetina*) (plate 7) blooms from mid-February through the summer. This is a perennial with bright yellow flowers and gray, woolly stems. Its name is derived from the flowers that persist and dry on the plant. Another sunflower on gravelly slopes of the foothills is **Mountain Heliopsis** or **Ox-eye** (*Heliopsis parvifolia*). This tall flower has naked stems and leaves with a rough texture. It is more frequent in late summer and fall.

The Mountains

Most of the mountain flowers are summertime bloomers only, but **Woolly Loco** (*Astragalus mollissimus*) (plate 9) can usually be found in flower along the Window Trail as early as February. Except during the driest part of summer, a few of these little purple plants can usually be found blooming somewhere in the mountains.

Phlox (*Phlox mesoleuca*) (plate 9) may bloom as early as March. Bright pink patches of these flowers can often be found along the roadsides on Panther Pass. And it isn't too long before **Stewart's Gilia**

(*Gilia stewartii*) (plate 9) is in bloom. This plant has lavender to purple flowers that may occur anywhere in the Chisos above 4,000 feet. **Hesper Mustard** (*Sisymbrium linearifolium*) is a common, showy, lavender flower that blooms from March through the fall months. And **Wood-sorrel** or **Sour-grass** (*Oxalis amplifolia*) (plate 9), an inconspicuous violet flower with cloverlike leaves, occurs in summer at moist places in the canyons.

Trompetilla or **Scarlet Bouvardia** (*Bouvardia ternifolia*) (plate 8) becomes the most common flowering plant of the pinyon-juniper woodlands by late summer. This woody member of the Madder Family is found only in West Texas and adjacent New Mexico and Mexico. **Snapdragon Vine** (*Maurandya antirrhiniflora*) produces red to violet flowers late in summer. I have found it most common in the canyons along the trail below Laguna Meadow. And consider yourself fortunate indeed if you find **Chisos Paintbrush** (*Castilleja elongata*) in bloom. This beautiful, red-flowering plant is endemic to these mountains.

One of the most fragile-appearing flowers of the mountains is **Blue** or **Prairie Flax** (*Linum lewisii*) (plate 9). Its blue flowers are common in early summer along the trail in upper Boot Canyon, and it occurs along roadsides at lower elevations as well. But of all the colorful mountain flowers, perhaps none is as beautiful as the **Mexican Campion** or **Catchfly** (*Silene laciniata*) (plate 9). This delicate plant, a member of the Pink Family, has bright red petals that are cleft into lobes.

Several common plants have white flowers, such as the **Texas Milkweed** (*Asclepias texana*) (plate 8), **Common Milkweed** (*A. elata*), **Wright's Eupatorium** (*Eupatorium wrightii*) (plate 8), and **Bigelow Bristlehead** (*Carpochaete bigelovii*). The first three are similar in appearance, but the last is usually much-branched and solitary, with five-petaled flowers that develop at the end of a short leafy branch. This is a common flower of the mountains in spring and early summer.

One of the most beautiful of the mountain flowers is **Longspur Columbine** (*Aquilegia longissima*) (plate 9) that is restricted to wet places along the lower edge of the mountain canyons and at Dripping Springs. This species occurs only in the Chisos Mountains and adjacent Mexico. It blooms during spring and early summer and is often replaced in fall by another real beauty, **Cardinal Flower** (*Lobelia cardinalis*). Tall red spikes of this plant bloom from summer until November.

Groundsel (*Senecio millelobatus*) is a common yellow flower that blooms quite early in the mountains. In fact, it may be the only yellow flower along the upper trails during April and May. In the mountains in summer grows a member of the Parsley Family, **Stemless Aletes** (*Aletes acaulis*), that is also common. This little plant bears a clump of yellow flowers on a long stem.

Buffalo-gourd or **Calabacilla Loca** (*Cucurbita foetidissima*) occurs in deeper soils of mountain flats. Its large yellow flowers may appear in late spring and summer, and the green to yellow fruits develop afterward. Indians used the round, two- to four-inch-long gourds for rattles.

By late summer the hillsides in the Basin and similar places begin to develop a golden hue from the abundance of late bloomers dominated by **Broomweed** or **Snakeweed** (*Xanthocephalum sphaerocephalum*). These plants may bloom locally until December. This plant is another indicator of disturbed soils. It will be interesting to find out if it decreases in abundance with the increasing return of native vegetation.

We cannot leave the discussion of yellow mountain flowers without mentioning the **Evening Primrose** (*Oenothera greggii*) (plate 9) that is common in spring and summer near the lodge, in upper Green Gulch, and elsewhere in the mountains. The flowers of this plant open in late afternoon and remain open until sunlight reaches them in the morning. Evening Primrose seems to be a favorite of bees, moths, and hummingbirds.

Plate 1

1. Texas Virgin's Bower
   Clematis drummondii
2. Tree Tobacco
   Nicotiana glauca
3. Bluebell
   Eustoma grandiflorum
4. Screwbean
   Prosopis pubescens
5. Honey Mesquite
   Prosopis glandulosa

6. Globe-mallow
   Sphaeralcea angustifolia
7. Silver-leaf Nightshade
   Solanum elaeagnifolium
8. Mexican Devil-weed
   Aster spinosus
9. Cowpen Daisy
   Verbesina encelioides

Plate 2

1. Mormon-tea
   Ephedra sp.
2. Guayacán
   Porlieria angustifolia
3. Squaw-bush
   Condalia spathulata
4. Tarbush
   Flourensia cernua
5. Mescat Acacia
   Acacia constricta

6. Catclaw Acacia
   Acacia berlandieri
7. Creosote Bush
   Larrea tridentata
8. Desert Willow
   Chilopsis linearis
9. Seepwillow
   Baccharis glutinosa

52

Plate 3

1. Allthorn
   Koeberlinia spinosa
2. Candelilla
   Euphorbia antisyphilitica
3. Lechuguilla
   Agave lecheguilla
4. Chisos Pricklypoppy
   Argemone chisosensis
5. Range Ratany
   Krameria glandulosa

6. False Agave
   Hechtia texensis
7. Ocotillo
   Fouquieria splendens
8. Rock-nettle
   Eucnide bartonioides
9. Leather Stem
   Jatropha dioica

53

Plate 4

1. Limincillo
   Pectis angustifolia
2. Desert Baileya
   Baileya multiradiata
3. Parralena
   Dyssodia pentachaeta
4. Chisos Bluebonnet
   Lupinus havardii
5. Desert Verbena
   Verbena wrightii

6. Gyp Phacelia
   Phacelia integrifolia
7. Trailing Allionia
   Allionia incarnata
8. Hillside Vervain
   Verbena neomexicana
9. Mesa Greggii
   Nerisyrenia camporum

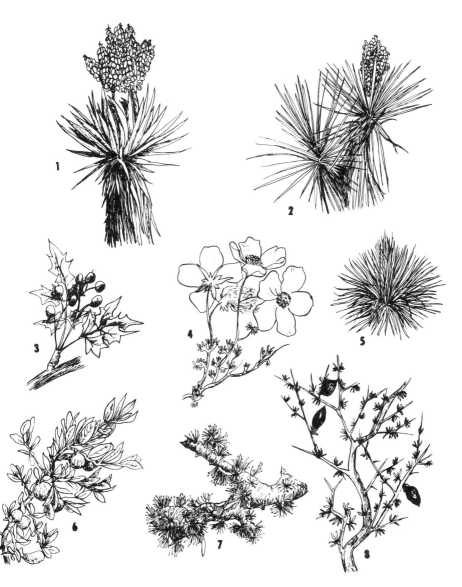

Plate 5

1. Giant Dagger
   Yucca carnerosana
2. Torrey Yucca
   Yucca torreyi
3. Agarito
   Berberis trifoliolata
4. Apache-Plume
   Fallugia paradoxa
5. Bear-grass
   Nolina erumpens
6. Texas Persimmon
   Diospyros texana
7. Desert Olive
   Forestiera angustifolia
8. Javelina Bush
   Condalia ericoides

55

Plate 6

1. Cat's-claw Mimosa
   Mimosa biuncifera
2. Catclaw
   Acacia roemeriana
3. Texas Mountain Laurel
   Sophora secundiflora
4. Silver-leaf
   Leucophyllum frutescens
5. Woolly Butterfly-bush
   Buddleja marrubiifolia

6. Feather Plume
   Dalea formosa
7. Antelope-horn
   Asclepias asperula
8. Zexmenia
   Zexmenia brevifolia
9. Resin-bush
   Viguiera stenoloba

56

Plate 7

1. Day-flower
   Commelina erecta
2. Braceted Paintbrush
   Castilleja latebracteata
3. Havard Penstemon
   Penstemon havardii
4. Woolly Paper-flower
   Psilostrophe tagetina
5. New Mexico Dalea
   Dalea neomexicana

6. Plains Black-foot
   Melampodium leucanthum
7. Bush Anisacantha
   Anisacanthus insignis
8. Mexican Poppy
   Kallstroemia grandiflora
9. Trumpet-flower
   Tecoma stans

57

Plate 8

1. Mountain Mahogany
   Cercocarpus montanus
2. Trompetilla
   Bouvardia ternifolia
3. Lead-tree
   Leucaena retusa
4. Texas Kidney Wood
   Eysenhardtia texana
5. Texas Milkweed
   Asclepias texana

6. Texas Buckeye
   Ungnadia speciosa
7. Damianita
   Chrysactinia mexicana
8. Mountain Sage
   Salvia regla
9. Wright's Eupatorium
   Eupatorium wrightii

Plate 9

1. Catchfly
   Silene laciniata
2. Longspur Columbine
   Aquilegia longissima
3. Woolly Loco
   Astragalus mollissimus
4. Phlox
   Phlox mesoleuca
5. Prairie Flax
   Linum lewisii

6. Stewart's Gilia
   Gilia stewartii
7. Evening Primrose
   Oenothera greggii
8. Common Horehound
   Marrubium vulgare
9. Wood-sorrel
   Oxalis amplifolia
10. Rock-trumpet
    Macrosiphonia macrosiphon

59

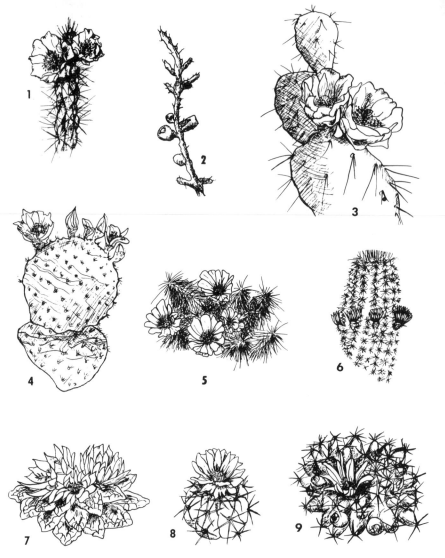

Plate 10

1. Cane Cholla
   Opuntia imbricata var.
   imbricata
2. Tasajillo
   Opuntia leptocaulis
3. Engelmann Prickly Pear
   Opuntia engelmannii
4. Blind Prickly Pear
   Opuntia rufida
5. Strawberry Cactus
   Echinocereus enneacanthus var.
   stramineus

6. Brown-flowered Cactus
   Echinocereus chloranthus var.
   chloranthus
7. Living Rock
   Ariocarpus fissuratus
8. Devil's Head
   Echinocactus horizonthalonius
9. Nipple Cactus
   Mammillaria meiacantha

60

6. The Cacti

THIS group of plants creates more interest than any other. In fact, many visitors to West Texas and Big Bend National Park plan their trip to see cacti at the peak of their blooming season. In most years this is early to mid-April when clumps of these spiny plants put on a show that even the most apathetic visitor appreciates.

No other national park has so many kinds of cacti or so many unique forms. More than seventy kinds have been recorded within the park, and a dozen more occur within less than an hour's driving time. The majority of Big Bend's cacti are desert dwellers, but several are grassland plants and a few are found only in the higher mountains.

Cacti may be divided into two distinct groups: those with glochids (**Chollas** and **Prickly Pears**) and those without glochids. Glochids are the tiny, barbed hairs or bristles that occur within areoles, the small depressions from which the spines emerge. Chollas have cylindrical stems that may branch into a dozen or more joints and may be from two or three inches to five or more feet tall. Prickly Pears possess flattened joints (pads) that also vary in structure and size. The following is an annotated list of most of the park's cacti.

Cane Cholla (*Opuntia imbricata* var. *imbricata*) (plate 10) is the common, sturdy cholla that occurs from the banks of the Rio Grande to the top of the mountains in the Big Bend Country. Stems are dull green, heavily imbricated, and very woody in character; dead skeletons are exceptionally decorative. Lavender to deep purple flowers appear during late spring, and yellowish fruits may persist throughout the winter.

Big Bend Cane Cholla (*Opuntia imbricata* var. *argentea*), although similar to Cane Cholla, is different enough to be considered as a distinct variety that is endemic to the dry limestone slopes of Mariscal Mountain. Numerous plants are visible from the River Road near Mariscal Mine. This plant differs from Cane Cholla in two ways: The spines are more numerous and silvery in color, and the overall appearance of the plant is lower and chubby.

Tasajillo (*Opuntia leptocaulis*) (plate 10) is one of the park's most common chollas. It is also known as **Pencil Cholla** and **Christmas Cactus**, the latter name derived from its bright red fruits that ripen in late fall and persist through the Christmas season. The stems of this plant are pencil-thin, and its half- to one-inch spines are usually covered with yellow sheaths.

Candle Cholla (*Opuntia kleiniae*) is larger than Tasajillo but smaller than Cane Cholla. This plant is found locally along the Rio Grande (it is fairly common between Castolon and Santa Elena Canyon) and a few places up to 5,200 feet. Its name is derived from the branched joints that may resemble a candelabra. Flowers are greenish, while those of Tasajillo are yellow.

Devil Cholla (*Opuntia schottii*) is one of the park's two ground chollas. This one forms large mats of spiny joints (two inches or longer) that break off very easily, becoming attached to anything that brushes against them. The plant may cover an area of several square yards. The long central spines are noticeably flattened in this plant, but the spines of the following species are round or only slightly flattened. These two plants apparently hybridize; it is easy to find plants with both characteristics.

Dog Cholla (*Opuntia grahamii*) is a smaller version of the above species and forms low mounds that are seldom more than three to four feet across. This plant is far more numerous in the park than Devil Cholla and occurs only within the Big Bend from near El Paso east through the park; Devil Cholla can be found along the Rio Grande from Brownsville to the western edge of the park. Both plants produce bright yellow flowers in spring.

Blind Prickly Pear (*Opuntia rufida*) (plate 10) is one of the few cacti entirely without spines. One of the park's most common species in the hot lowlands, it is also particularly abundant on limestone cliffs near Boquillas Canyon. This erect and somewhat bushy plant may grow to a height of six feet. The pads are dark gray-green in color, and the large areoles contain brownish-red to chocolate brown glochids. Lemon yellow flowers appear during April and early May.

Grassland Prickly Pear (*Opuntia macrorhiza*) is an inconspicuous plant that occurs infrequently in the mountains, where it forms low (three to six inches high), spreading, loose clumps within the grasslands. The pads are small and bluish-green in color, and one to three spines grow from the upper areoles. Faint rosy-red flowers occur only occasionally in early summer.

Dark-spined Prickly Pear (*Opuntia atrispina*) is a sprawling, but erect cactus that occurs only in the Texas Big Bend Country. I have found it only a few times in the Chisos foothills. Spines, which grow only from the upper areoles, are black at the base and shade to gray or tan. The yellow flowers that bloom in April or May are quite short-lived.

Englemann Prickly Pear (*Opuntia engelmannii*) (plate 10) is the common Prickly Pear throughout the Southwest. It is an extremely variable plant that hybridizes readily with *Opuntia phaecantha*, producing a wide range of plants. This species possesses rather thick, green to blue-green pads that may be spreading or bushy with a defined trunk. Some plants, such as those on the Rio Grande Village Nature Trail, may be six to eight feet tall. Areoles are widely separated and contain three or four rather short spines that may be white or brownish in color. The longer ones are usually bent and somewhat flattened. Bright yellow flowers appear in spring and early summer and the fruits, which are large and deep purple when ripe, make excellent jams and jellies.

Brownspine Prickly Pear (*Opuntia phaecantha*) is as variable as the above species. Plants may be erect or prostrate but are seldom more than three feet in height. The pads are usually longer than broad, dull green to grayish green, and rather thick, with brownish areoles that are separated by as much as an inch. The clusters of one to four spines on the side of the pads are mostly bent downward, while those on the edge of the pads are longer and straighter. Spines may be whitish to yellow or brown to reddish. Flowers are golden yellow with a yellow to reddish center.

Spinyfruit Prickly Pear (*Opuntia phaeacantha* var. *spinosibacca*) is an endemic plant that was described by Margery Anthony as late as 1956. It is abundant on the limestone hills between Boquillas Canyon and Rio Grande Village. Its light green pads possess numerous light yellow to dark yellow spines that may be twisted or straight. Short-lived yellow flowers bloom in April or May, and the fruits are very spiny (thus the name of the plant).

Chisos Prickly Pear (*Opuntia lindheimeri* var. *chisosensis*) is the common, yellow-spined Prickly Pear of the Chisos Mountains. It is a spreading plant that rarely exceeds three feet in height. The grayish-green pads contain widely spaced areoles with yellow glochids and yellow spines that may be two and a half inches in length. Yellow flowers bloom in profusion during late spring and early summer.

Cow's Tongue Prickly Pear (*Opuntia lindheimeri* var. *linguiformis*) is not native to the park but occurs at several places in the lowlands where it apparently was introduced by early settlers. It is easy to identify by its thin, elongated, "tonguelike" pads that contain widely separated areoles with brown glochids and slender yellow spines. Golden yellow flowers bloom in late spring.

Purple-Tinged Prickly Pear (*Opuntia macrocentra*) is an easy-to-identify plant because of its purplish pads and very long spines (*macrocentra* means long-spine). The purple tinge is greatest around the areoles and on the edges, although the entire plant may be purple in winter. It may be bushy or spreading and seldom is more than three feet tall. Numerous bright yellow flowers, with red centers, appear during spring. This plant is most prevalent in the lowlands but may be found up to 4,000 feet elevation.

The second group of Big Bend cacti are those that do not possess glochids. It includes a variety of forms whose nomenclature is as varied as the authors. The following is a key to the genera of this group, based upon Del Weniger's (1970) classification:

Vegetative Key to Cacti other than Opuntia of Big Bend

1a Stems of mature plants are ribbed—2
1b Stems of mature plants are smooth or else tubercled—5
    2a Plants possess spines—3
    2b Plants are spineless .... *Lophophora*
        3a Flowers are produced on the sides of stems—4
        3b Flowers are produced at the apex
        of stems .... *Echinocactus*
            4a Flowers are produced from a rupture of
            the stem just above an areole .... *Echinocereus*
            4b Flowers are produced from within a
            spine areole .... *Cereus*
            5a Plants possess spines—6
            5b Plants are spineless .... *Ariocarpus*

6a Flowers are produced in the
    axils of tubercles . . . . *Mammillaria*
6b Flowers are produced from
    the tips of the tubercles . . . . *Epithelantha*

Night-Blooming Cereus (*Cereus greggii*) is the park's only cactus that flowers after dark. This species is rare in the park, but with luck can be located in spring by its sweet-smelling white blossoms. It may be more common than is evident because the square stems are easily broken by animals and therefore many plants may not be readily visible. The root is the major part of the plant; it may be as much as two feet in diameter and weigh up to 125 pounds.

Green-flowered Cactus (*Echinocereus viridiflorus* var. *cylindricus*) is a northern plant that reaches the southern edge of its range within the park. It is a common cactus of the rolling hills of the Davis and Del Norte mountains, but I have found it only once in the park—above Ash Spring on the north side of Vernon Bailey Peak. This compact, cylindrical plant is seldom more than six inches high. Although it possesses several radial spines, it is usually without a central spine. One of the best characteristics for identification is the elongated areoles. Greenish to reddish-brown flowers appear on the sides of the plant.

Brown-flowered Cactus (*Echinocereus chloranthus* var. *chloranthus*) (plate 10) is one of the park's most abundant cacti below 5,000 feet elevation. It prefers igneous soils and may be found on the banks of the Rio Grande from Santa Elena Canyon to Glenn Springs and north to Dagger Flat and Study Butte. This plant is similar to the previous species but has round areoles and may be ten inches tall. Flowers appear on the sides of the plant during spring and may be greenish to a deep reddish-brown. Spines vary in length from a few millimeters to almost one and a quarter inches.

Yellow-flowered Cactus (*Echinocereus chloranthus* subsp.) is yet another plant of this complex. It occurs infrequently on rocky slopes and in protected side canyons of the Chisos Mountains. It may be eight inches tall, with long central spines that may be two and a half inches in length and greenish-yellow flowers that appear on the sides.

Chisos Pitaya (*Echinocereus chisosensis*) is one of Big Bend National Park's endemic cacti. This one occurs on the open desert flats in the southeastern part of the park, above 2,400 feet elevation, and usually is found growing with another plant, such as a living or dead Lechuguilla. Taller plants may be fourteen inches. It may be solitary or branched into three to six stems that are cylindrical but somewhat pointed at the top. The stem is easily visible because the spines are relatively short. The areoles always contain cottony materials. Flowers bloom during March and April and are fuchsia colored with a cream to white center and green stigma.

Ashy-white Pitaya (*Echinocereus pectinatus* var. *wenigeri*) may be exotic to Big Bend National Park; the inclusion of this cactus here is based upon a single plant I found near Gano Spring. This is a beautiful cactus with short white spines that arise from oval areoles that are woolly, particularly at the top of the plant. Although I have never seen its flowers, Weniger (1970) illustrates this plant with a large pink-flowering specimen.

Slender-spined Pitaya (*Echinocereus pectinatus* var. *minor*) is common in the park only on the Mesa de Anguila, but it is also present on Dagger Flat and along Tornillo Creek. The plant may be fourteen inches tall, with pink and gray bands like **Texas Rainbow**. Spines are shorter and more slender in this plant, however, making the ribs more obvious. Flower color is different, too. These flowers are magenta, while those of other forms of the species are yellow.

Rio Grande Pitaya (*Echinocereus pectinatus* var. *pectinatus*) occurs only along the rocky banks of the Rio Grande in the park. I have often found it between Santa Elena Canyon and Reed Camp. A specimen from near Reed Camp was brought to park headquarters in February, 1967, where it produced yellow flowers in April, 1970. This is a fine-spined plant with rather delicate features.

Texas Rainbow Pitaya (*Echinocereus pectinatus* var. *neomexicanus*) is the most common plant of this group and occurs almost everywhere in the park below 4,000 feet elevation. This is the plant that many botanists refer to as *Echinocereus dasyacanthus*. It may be sixteen inches tall, be solitary or clumped in two to ten stems, and produce large yellow to cream flowers during late spring. It is possible to confuse small individuals with the common **Brown-flowered Cactus**, but Texas Rainbow flowers occur on spiny stems that appear near the top of the plant.

Big Bend Pitaya (*Echinocereus pectinatus* subsp.) is similar to

Echinocereus ctenoides but is banded with pink and gray like the above cactus. It occurs in the park in a rather small area between Oak Creek and Croton Spring and on Burro Mesa, where it is quite common. Stems may be solitary or branched into ten to fifteen stems that may be fourteen inches tall. There are no central spines, and radials hide the stems, which are noticeably ridged. Bright yellow flowers with greenish bases to the petals appear during spring.

Little Claret-cup (*Echinocereus triglochidiatus* var. *melanacanthus*) is present in small numbers throughout the Chisos Mountains. This is the clumping variety of the species, and as many as 500 tuberculated stems may occur together. Each stem is three to six inches in length, and the one to three central spines are half as long as the five to eleven radials. Flowers are rather short and reddish, fading to cream or light yellow at the base of the petals.

Southwest Claret-cup (*Echinocereus triglochidiatus* var. *neomexicanus*) is fairly common in the park. It forms small clumps of five to forty-five stems that are eight to twelve inches in height. The two to four central spines are about twice as long as the nine to twelve radials. Flowers of this plant are longer than those of the previous cactus and are all bright red, without the lighter centers.

Texas Claret-cup (*Echinocereus triglochidiatus* var. *gurneyi*) is the most common variety of this species in the park. Like the two previous plants, it is confined to the mountains and hills above 3,400 feet elevation. This cactus seldom clumps, but branched stems to twelve inches are not uncommon. The one (rarely two) central spine is about the same length as the seven to nine radials. Flowers are similar to those of Little Claret-cup, but larger.

Warty Hedgehog (*Echinocereus enneacanthus* var. *enneacanthus*) is found in silty soils only along the river from Boquillas to Santa Elena Canyon. Mature plants may occur as slightly elevated clumps of as many as 100 or more stems. The large stems are very flabby when touched with a foot or a stick and are easily broken. Light red flowers appear during spring; they are not as dark or as dense as **Strawberry Cactus** flowers.

Strawberry Cactus (*Echinocereus enneacanthus* var. *stramineus*) (plate 10) is one of the park's most prominent species in the desert lowlands. Strawberry Cactus is abundant at Persimmon Gap, Dagger Flat, near Maverick, and many other places in the park. It is easily identified because of its habit of forming mounds of stems that may be three feet high and four feet wide. The straw-colored spines are so numerous that they usually hide the stems. Bright red flowers bloom during spring and summer, and the fruits are large and delicious when ripe. In fact, the fruits can be eaten alone or with milk and sugar like strawberries; hence, the common name.

Strawberry Hedgehog (*Echinocereus enneacanthus* var. *dubius*) looks very much like the previous cactus but does not grow in an elevated mound. It has gray to tan spines, and the fruits are not nearly as tasty as those of Strawberry Cactus. This plant is common on desert flats, where it may be five feet across. On Tornillo Flat you can find this plant on open silty areas and the Strawberry Cactus on nearby rocky outcroppings. Flowers are similar, too, but are not as bright and have fewer petals.

Devil's Head (*Echinocactus horizonthalonius*) (plate 10) is another of Big Bend's common cacti that occurs within the mountains and flats below 4,800 feet elevation. It is found only in West Texas. This smooth-ribbed, globular-shaped plant may be as tall as twelve inches, although most plants are five to eight inches tall. Stout but flattened reddish spines occur along each broad, gray-green rib. Deep purple to light pink flowers appear at the top center of the plant during spring and after summer rains. This is one of the little "barrel" cacti that are swiftly disappearing outside the park because commercial cactus dealers are gathering them.

Devil's Claw (*Echinocactus texensis*) is similar to Devil's Head but occurs in entirely different habitats. This species prefers deep clay and silty soils along the river and on higher flats such as Tornillo or Dog Canyon. Although it is never abundant, a little searching in the proper habitat will usually reveal several. Ranchers call this plant the "horse crippler" because it grows so low in the soil that a passing horse may not see it until he runs into its stout, sharp spines. The visible part of the stem appears rather flattened because most of the globular stem is below the surface. The ribs are not as smooth as Devil's Head and the spines are fewer, stouter, and deflexed downward against the ribs. Flowers of this plant are not as showy as those of the previous species, being smaller and pale pink in color.

Catclaw Cactus (*Echinocactus uncinatus* var. *wrightii*) is one of the park's "fish-hooked" cacti. This one is widespread from the limestone soils along the Rio Grande to 6,500 feet in the Chisos Mountains, the top of the Dead Horse and Mariscal mountains, and Mesa de Anguila. It is rarely more than seven inches high and possesses thirteen strongly tubercled ribs from which the spines protrude. The central spine is long and hooked, yellowish below and reddish above. Reddish-brown flowers appear in a circle near the top of the stem in spring and after heavy summer rains.

Tobusch Cactus (*Echinocactus tobuschii*) was known from only a few plants found in Bandera County, Texas, until I found it in the Dead Horse Mountains. It certainly is one of the rarest of Texas cacti, although it is possible that it is more common than is recognized, since its resemblance to immature Turk's Head may lead to mistaken identification of it. The plant is rarely more than five inches tall, and its dark green stem is at least partly hidden by many spines. Each prominent tubercle has seven to twelve short radials and three to five central spines. The upper two centrals are straight and turned upward forming a V, but the lower one is hooked and ridged and stands out from the stem. Mature spines are gray at the base and turning maroon to red at the tip. Flowers are yellow-green and bloom during the spring; one collected in mid-February produced flowers on March 18 and May 29.

Turk's Head (*Echinocactus hamatacanthus*) is the park's largest native "barrel" cactus and is widespread from the banks of the Rio Grande to 7,000 feet elevation in the Chisos Mountains. This large, hook-spined plant is found along the gravel banks of the river, hanging on bare limestone cliffs in the canyons, and on rocky outcroppings in the Chisos Basin. It is usually solitary, but plants with two to ten stems are not uncommon. Bright yellow flowers appear during summer and fall, and greenish fruits may persist on the plants all winter.

Southwestern Barrel Cactus (*Echinocactus wislizeni*) has been found near ruins of houses along the river where it undoubtedly was planted in the past. This is an exotic species to the park; its nearest natural occurrence is in the mountains near El Paso and westward. Southwestern Barrel is a typical barrel cactus with very prominent ribs on globular to cylindrical stems. Spines are variable, but the centrals are stout, flattened, and strongly hooked. The yellow to red flowers form a circle around the top of the plant.

Bicolor Cactus (*Thelocactus bicolor* var. *schottii*) is an extraordinary plant that occurs locally between Hot Springs and the Johnson

Ranch along the river. It usually grows solitary as a globular to oval plant that may be fourteen inches tall. Its bluish green to gray stems are hidden by a mass of variable spines that may be round or flattened and yellow to reddish in color. Flowers vary, too; some are brilliant purple-red, while others are light pink with a cream to yellowish center.

Woven-spine Pineapple Cactus (*Echinocactus intertextus* var. *intertextus*) is very rare in Big Bend National Park but is common in the grasslands of the Davis Mountains. I have found it only twice within the park: near Ward Spring and on Burro Mesa. It is an interesting little plant, seldom more than five inches tall, with many stout spines that are tightly pressed against the round body of the stem. One can pick up this plant and handle it without discomfort. Flowers are relatively small and white to cream in color.

White-flowered Cactus (*Echinocactus erectocentrus* var. *pallidus*) is as abundant as the previous plant is rare. This little cactus is found on all of the gravelly hills along the river, up to 3,500 feet in the Chisos Mountains and higher in the Dead Horse, Mariscal, and Rattlesnake mountains. It is the earliest cactus in the park to bloom; I have found several blooming as early as February 28 along Fresno Creek. Most plants are solitary and two to four inches high, although larger plants are common on Burro Mesa. This plant differs from the previous cactus in that its central spines protrude from the stem, although the radials are pressed against the stem like the above variety. Flowers are large and white.

Mariposa Cactus (*Echinocactus mariposensis*) occurs only rarely in the park but is common in the vicinity of Terlingua where it was first discovered. In fact, the name is derived from Terlingua's Mariposa Mine, the type locality. This is another of the little round cacti with many white radial spines that hide the stems. The central spines spread upward and are gray to yellowish at the base, fading to blue or reddish color. Flowers are whitish with green midribs.

Warnock's Cactus (*Echinocactus warnocki*) looks very much like Mariposa Cactus but some differences do distinguish the two—the radial spines of Warnock's Cactus are finer and the flowers are larger and violet in color. This plant has only recently been described by Benson (1969), who named it *Neolloydia warnocki* after Dr. Barton Warnock of Sul Ross State University, who was the first to collect it. However, it is so

The Window and Terlingua area from the Pinnacles Trail.

Green Gulch and Casa Grande.

Fall in the Chisos, looking toward Mt. Emory from the Laguna Meadows Trail.

Looking southeast across the Boot toward Mexico's Sierra del Carmens.

close to the above species that I have included it here. It is locally common on little open flats on Mariscal and the Dead Horse mountains from 2,500 to 4,000 feet elevation.

Texas Cactus (*Echinocactus conoideus*) is abundant on the dry limestone slopes of the Dead Horse Mountains. This plant is also known as *Neolloydia texensis*. It is a conical-shaped plant that may be ten inches high, although most plants are shorter. Indistinct ribs form low rows of tubercles on the gray-green stem, which is fairly well hidden by white to gray radial spines. The centrals are stouter and blackish in color. Very showy reddish-purple flowers appear in spring and after summer rains.

Peyote (*Lophophora williamsii*) is one of the rarest of cacti, occurring in the park only near old Indian sites. It is possible that all of the park's plants were introduced by Indians, who used the plants in religious ceremonies. Used since pre-Columbian days, Peyote gained recent recognition because of its use as a hallucinogen. In spite of being protected within the national park and unlawful elsewhere, Peyote is fast disappearing from its former range within the Rio Grande Valley from Presidio to the lower valley. This species is a little, rounded cactus with gray-green tubercles that lack spines. Small pink flowers, borne in the top center of the stem, appear in spring and after summer rains.

Living Rock (*Ariocarpus fissuratus*) (plate 10) is well named because it looks more like a rock or a piece of gray bone than a living plant. It may be up to six inches wide but is so flat against the ground that it takes a trained eye to find one. The surface is warty and fissured, and the center is usually filled with cotton. The bright pink blooms, which appear in fall during October and early November, are quite large for the size of the plant. Living Rocks grow only in the lowlands of northern Mexico and adjacent Texas within an area from Presidio to the Pecos River and north to Alpine. It is one of the park's most unusual plants.

Button Cactus (*Epithelantha micromeris*) is a petite little cactus with tiny spines that are tightly pressed against the stem. It is rarely more than an inch high and half as wide. The spines are so small that this plant can be picked up between the thumb and forefinger without pricking the skin. It is very similar to the following species and resembles a little spherical button. Button Cactus occurs only in West Texas and is found in the park only in the western corner on the Mesa de Anguila and near Lajitas. The flowers are pinkish and half an inch in length.

Boquillas Button Cactus (*Epithelantha bokei*) is known only from the limestone slopes of the Dead Horse Mountains near Boquillas north to Dog Canyon. It is very similar to the previous cactus but is somewhat smaller, and its flowers are white rather than being pink like those of the Button Cactus. This little plant blends in so well with the layered limestone that it is almost impossible to see at first.

Sea-urchin Cactus (*Mammillaria echinus*) occurs in a limited area of West Texas and is fairly common on limestone soils of the Dead Horse and Mariscal mountains and on Mesa de Anguila. Most plants are solitary, but clumps with only a few to as many as fifteen stems do occur. Stems are seldom more than six inches tall, round or egg-shaped, and fairly well hidden by the spines. The numerous radials grow pressed against the stem, while the lowest of the three or four thicker central spines stands straight out from the center of the spine cluster. Very noticeable yellow flowers bloom in summer after each rainstorm.

Big Bend Mammillaria (*Mammillaria ramillosa*) is another of the unusual cacti found in the Texas Big Bend. This one has been located only along the Rio Grande in Brewster and Terrell counties and in adjacent Mexico. It is difficult to find because it occurs on isolated limestone slopes west of Mariscal Mountain in the park and east to Reagan Canyon. The plant, rarely more than three inches tall, is shaped like a cone. It bears many gray to black, slender radial spines that may be pressed against the stem or curving upward and four slender, brown to black central spines that stand out away from the stem. Flowers are red-purple and bloom during late spring and after heavier summer storms.

Long Mamma (*Mammillaria macromeris*) occurs on clay flats and gravelly slopes up to 3,500 feet elevation. It has a variety of forms; I have found plants that are solitary or in a cluster of 2 or 3, and others that may be in clusters of more than 100 stems. This cactus is easy to identify because of the loose characteristic of the stems and the long (one-half to one and a half inches), soft tubercles over the entire plant. Gray to black spines, which may be two inches in length, are borne from the areole near the tip of each tubercle. Deep pink to purple flowers bloom during summer and early fall.

Bisquit Cactus (*Mammillaria vivipara* var. *radiosa*) is a mountain cactus that is fairly common on the slopes below Mount Emory and less numerous within the lower pinyon-juniper woodlands. It is seldom more than two inches tall and usually solitary in occurrence. Its areoles are large for the size of the plant and noticeably woolly. White radial spines are pressed against the stem, but the four to six centrals are stouter, brownish, and swollen at the base. Flowers are greenish to brown and appear during summer. Fruits are green. This neat little mountain plant usually goes unnoticed because of its habit of growing among the litter of the mountain woodlands.

Fragrant Cactus (*Mammillaria fragrans*) is a rare cactus of the lower foothills and gravelly banks adjacent to the Rio Grande and is restricted to the Texas Big Bend. Plants may be eight inches tall and possess dull gray stems with numerous and somewhat flattened tubercles. Twenty to thirty radials and six to twelve central spines that are brown to maroon in color spread out at all angles. Flowers are rather large and reddish-purple.

Cob Cactus (*Mammillaria tuberculosa*) is one of the park's most common cacti, occurring on the cliffs along the Rio Grande to the upper parts of the Chisos Mountains. It may be solitary or much branched at the base to form clumps of two to fifteen stems that are seldom more than ten inches tall. The gray-green stems are well hidden by the short and variable spines except at the base of the plant, where spines fall off the older tubercles. The bare tubercles become quite corky with age. The violet-pink flowers are borne on the tips of the stems during April and May and again after summer rains.

Mountain Cob Cactus (*Mammillaria dasyacantha*) is very similar to Cob Cactus but may be much larger (to fourteen inches) and does not have bare tubercles around the base of the stem. This species grows with Bisquit Cactus in the mountain woodlands and with Cob Cactus in the rocky parts of the mountains and adjacent grasslands down to approximately 3,000 feet elevation. It is the most common cactus of rocky slopes of the Chisos foothills. Flowers are white to pale pink, with a bright green stigma.

White-spine Cob Cactus (*Mammillaria albicolumnaria*) is another of the little columnar plants known as the genus *Escobaria* to some botanists. This cactus is the least known and is restricted to limestone soils near Boquillas, on Mariscal Mountain, and on the Mesa de Anguila. Some stems may be ten inches tall and are well hidden by numerous very white spines (with pinkish tips) that seem to radiate in all directions. Flowers of this species are brighter pink and larger than Cob Cactus and bloom in April and May after summer rains.

Varicolor Cactus (*Mammillaria varicolor*) is another of the park's rare little cacti. This one has been found only a few times in the foothills of the Chisos Mountains. Its very delicate spines only partially hide the dainty green stems. Radial spines are numerous (fifteen to twenty), very thin, and white; the four to five centrals are a little heavier and, except for the lowest one that stands outward, lie next to the stem. Flowers are white to pinkish and are similar to those of the Mountain Cob Cactus.

Duncan's Cactus (*Mammillaria duncanii*) is one of the most inconspicuous of cacti. It grows in crevices on limestone cliffs in only a few isolated places near Terlingua and from Mariscal Mountain to Boquillas. This species, rarely more than an inch in height, often passes for an immature Cob Cactus. Flowers, however, are pink and considerably larger than those of Cob Cactus, and almost hide this little plant.

Foxtail Cactus (*Mammillaria pottsii*) is found only in the western corner of the park. It is fairly common on the dry limestone hills near Terlingua and on the Mesa de Anguila. The cylindrical stems of this pretty little plant are rarely more than six inches tall and may be solitary or clumped. The stems are hidden by short, white to reddish radial spines, and six to twelve gray, dark-tipped centrals that are longer and stouter and protrude out and upward. Reddish to light purple flowers appear in a rosette near the top of the stem in spring and after summer rains.

Golf-ball Cactus (*Mammillaria lasiacantha*) grows on limestone slopes from Boquillas to Dog Canyon in the Dead Horse Mountains, on Mariscal Mountain and Mesa de Anguila, and adjacent flats. It grows with Button Cacti and looks very much like them at first sight. Rarely more than one and a half inches high, this fine-spined plant produces a little white ball of delicate spines that looks like a golf ball. Flowers vary somewhat from white to pink, with a purplish-red midstrip on each petal. Plants on the extreme western part of the park produce darker pink flowers, while those of the rest of the area have white flowers; it is possible that there is a varietal difference.

Pancake Pincushion (*Mammillaria heyderi* var. *applanata*) is a flat plant with large tubercles containing ten to eighteen white radials and one central spine. This is the low-growing *Mammillaria* of limestone soils occurring from Tornillo Flat to the silty soils along the Rio Grande. I have never found it on igneous soils. Flowers occur in a rosette and are creamy white with a green midrib.

Nipple Cactus (*Mammillaria meiacantha*) (plate 10) is similar to the previous plant but possesses heavier spines and grows only on igneous soils from the alluvial gravels along the river to the top of the Chisos Mountains. This is a common species of the rocky alluvial fans of the foothills. Flowers are similar to the previous plant but are white rather than creamy.

7. Mammals

THERE are no chipmunks in Big Bend National Park, but more kinds of mammals do occur there than most people would guess. However, since the majority of the park's mammals are nocturnal, they are not often observed by park visitors. If you are interested in seeing mammals, you must drive the desert roads at dusk and just before dawn, when they are most active. A drive from the Chisos Basin, down Green Gulch, and west to Maverick or Sotol Vista would undoubtedly reveal at least a few of Big Bend's seventy-five kinds of mammals.

Two species of deer can be found within the park. The mountain deer is the **Sierra del Carmen Whitetail**. It prefers the woodland environment and is rarely seen below 5,000 feet elevation. A relatively small deer, without the huge ears of the **Mule Deer**, Whitetails are gray-brown in color, with the characteristic flag tail that is especially prominent when the deer is frightened. Mule Deer are common in the lowlands below 5,000 feet. This is a larger animal without the flag tail, although the rump and upper part of the tail are white. Antler shapes differ in the two species; those of the Mule Deer fork into equal branches, while the antler branches of the Whitetail bucks all develop off one beam.

Deer are grazers and often feed along roadsides where grass may be greener because of the extra moisture held beneath the road surface. It may appear that deer are more numerous outside the park than within it, but this is not necessarily true. Outside the park deer vie with stock for feed away from the roadways, and so they move to areas outside fenced ranchlands where there is less competition.

Coyotes are nighttime wanderers, and it is not uncommon to see one or more of these predators in the glare of your headlights at night. This dog is one of the few of our larger predators that seem to have adapted to civilization, in spite of being persecuted by ranchers. Coyotes have learned to hunt the roadways for road kills; they seldom go hungry. The lonesome cry of a coyote is a distinctive feature of the desert at night. They are usually quiet during the summer months.

However, from September through April, if you stop along the desert road at night, climb out of your vehicle, and listen for a few minutes, you will certainly hear the calls of coyotes. It is a sound that may chill you at first, but when it becomes familiar you will look forward to the nocturnal choruses; and if you leave the desert, you will miss it.

Two, possibly three, other Canids occur in the park, and, like the Coyote, are nocturnal predators. The **Kit Fox** is a tiny desert fox that is rarely seen at elevations above 3,500 feet. The **Gray Fox** is relatively common almost everywhere in the park. This is the little dog you are likely to see on an after-dark drive. Its long, dark gray tail and short, reddish ears make this one of the most handsome animals of the Big Bend.

The **Gray** or **Mexican Wolf** was long considered extirpated from Texas, but recent records in West Texas state that two of these wolves were shot by hunters north of the park, suggesting that this magnificent animal may make a comeback. The presence of wolves clearly illustrates the wilderness character of the country. The recovery of a wolf population, if it occurs, would be definite evidence of the restoration of Big Bend National Park to conditions as they were before the appearance of the Europeans and cattle.

Another nighttime wanderer, and one that you are likely to see, is the **Collared Peccary** or **Javelina** (Have-ah-LEE-nah). These little native pigs are surprisingly common in Big Bend National Park. Although they are most active at night, you may be able to find javelinas in the foothill arroyos during the daytime as well. I have seen them most often along the Grapevine Hills Road, in Panther and Ash Creek canyons, and behind the Old Ranch. Because they are so shortsighted, you may be able to approach quite near to one before being detected. Don't be confused by the musky scent that is similar to the smell of a skunk. Javelinas do not use their scent for defense; rather, it is for recognition by other javelinas and to mark their territories. The scent gland is situated on the rump, two or three inches above the tail, but low enough so that the javelina can rub the gland against rocks and shrubs or other javelinas. Scent plays a very important role in their detection of friends and enemies. Javelinas are very curious, yet have very poor eyesight; a hiker who stumbles upon a small band of them may think he is being attacked if he is approached by a curious boar or sow, but he is merely being investigated.

The odor of a javelina is almost exactly like that of a skunk; it takes

The Javelina is North America's only native pig. These animals are fairly common in Big Bend National Park and can most easily be found by searching after dark along the roadways. NPS photo by Evans.

considerable experience to tell them apart. Both mammals can usually be found by driving the roads at night. Big Bend National Park has four kinds of skunks, all nocturnal animals that feed upon insects, small reptiles, rodents, and birds and their eggs. The smallest of these is the **Spotted Skunk**. This species and the larger and more numerous **Striped Skunk** are widely distributed, and you are as likely to find one along the river as in the higher canyons of the Chisos Mountains. The **Hooded** and **Hog-nosed** skunks are more restricted. The latter species occurs only in the mountains; it has a piglike snout, and its back and tail are usually all white. The Hooded Skunk is found primarily in the lowlands. It is usually all black but may have faint white lines along the side of the body. In some years park rangers have difficulty controlling the population of skunks in the Chisos Basin. When these nighttime wanderers become too numerous, the rangers trap them alive and transfer them to less densely inhabited regions of the park.

The **Badger** is another nocturnal predator. Evidence of these short but streamlined mammals is found regularly, but you are not likely to see one on a nighttime drive. Their nearest relative is the **Raccoon**. Although raccoons are seldom seen, you can find their tracks at almost any muddy place in the park from the river to the mountain springs.

The cat family is represented in the park by two species, the **Bobcat** and the **Mountain Lion** or **Panther**. The first and smallest of the two is fairly common throughout the park, although it has a remarkable ability to go unseen. After I had lived at Panther Junction for three years without seeing a bobcat there, one day at noon one of these animals suddenly appeared, lying in the grass near a watering tank. I watched it from only ten feet away all during the noon hour. It was gone as swiftly as it had appeared. I have not seen one there since.

The mountain lion or panther is Big Bend's most famous cat. Several places have been named after this large mammal: Panther Junction, Panther Peak, Panther Pass, Panther Canyon, and Panther Spring. And park residents named their softball and basketball teams of 1969, 1970, and 1971 the Pink Panthers. If it is possible to identify the best place to see this great cat in the park, I would suggest Panther Pass, since more mountain lions have been reported in that area, but Panther Pass is also one of the most heavily visited areas of the park. The majority of the sightings are recorded during May and June.

How many mountain lions occur within the park? Roy McBride (1977) has provided some information about lion populations along the Texas-Mexican border that is more than speculation. He spent sixteen years studying lions before writing a thesis on the subject for a master's degree at Sul Ross State University in Alpine. He estimated that the Big Bend National Park population was twenty-one animals in 1976, with an additional sixty-four animals in the rest of Brewster County. His thesis has provided a great deal of valuable and surprising information about the habits of desert lions. Some of his information contradicts long-standing beliefs; for example, he describes a herd of Mule Deer on a ranch in southeast Brewster County:

> A limestone hill between the ranch headquarters and a windmill served as a browsing area for four doe mule deer. They frequently could be seen in the same area and were very gentle. One of the does had been shot

through the front leg but had somehow managed to live. She was unable to run and just hobbled around with the other does as best she could. A female lion moved into the area and in a 60-day period killed the three healthy does but not the crippled one. This doe remained in the same region until she disappeared, many months later. I assumed that she died and I later found her carcass (uneaten) not far from the site where she always stayed.

She would have been easy prey for the lion, but I can only assume that because of her poor condition, the lion did not want her. In view of these facts, it seems that a lion's function in a deer herd is not simply to weed out the sick or crippled, but to suppress the overall deer herd. [pp. 101–102]

McBride's thesis, which will be published by the National Park Service, is important in understanding predator-prey relations.

Big Bend National Park is left alone so that its native vegetation can return to the conditions existing before the establishment of ranches. Today, the park contains a naturally regulated population of predators and prey. The deer population needs no reduction or artificial control. Mountain Lions are important factors in such a situation. There are few places where the "balance of nature" functions as well as it does in the park.

On dry spring and summer nights when the moon is not too bright, six to eight species of rodents may be found along the roadway. The tiny animal that you may see running across the road in front of your approaching vehicle is the **Apache Pocket Mouse.** Two *Perognathus* species, the **Desert** and **Nelson's** pocket mice, also occur in the park. The last species possesses spinelike hair on the rump.

The kangaroo rat you are likely to see as you drive in the desert is **Merriam's Kangaroo Rat.** However, at patches of heavier vegetation along the river and near Tornillo Creek, you may find **Ord's Kangaroo Rat.** These "Dipos" are about the same size and difficult to separate in the field, but a closer examination will reveal that Merriam's has four toes on each back foot while Ord's may have either four or five, and the tail stripe is much broader than that of *Dipodomys merriami.*

Other nighttime rodents include five species of *Peromyscus* (*P. eremicus, maniculatus, leucopus, boylii,* and *pectoralis*), the **Western** and **Fulvous Harvest Mouse, Southern Grasshopper Mouse,** three wood rats (*Neotoma micropus, albigula,* and *mexicana*), and two cotton rats (*Sigmodon hisipidus* and *ochrognathus*). The latter species — **Yellow-nosed Cotton Rat** — is restricted to only a few grassy areas in

The White-throated Wood Rat is common throughout the park, but its nocturnal habits make it one of the least frequently seen mammals. Photo by Porter.

The Yellow-nosed Cotton Rat has increased in numbers since the establishment of the park. It frequents stipa grass flats within the Chisos Mountains. Photo by Porter.

the park and in southwest New Mexico and adjacent Arizona. John Baccus studied this species and other small mammals of the Big Bend Park grasslands during 1970 and 1971, and he found that the Yellow-nosed Cotton Rat was a good indicator of the condition of the grasslands, since it chooses only undisturbed areas as a habitat. The range of this species has increased considerably since the time when the Chisos Mountains were ranchlands.

Bats make up more than one-quarter of the list of the park's mammals. Nineteen species of these flying insect eaters were recorded by David Easterla during the summers of 1967 through 1972. His most surprising discovery was the **Spotted Bat**, a first for Texas. Mammalogists had previously found this rare mammal only in forested places in Arizona, New Mexico, and southern Utah. The presence of adults in the limestone hills of Big Bend caused Easterla to theorize that Spotted Bats are cliff-roosting species rather than tree-dwelling, which previously was accepted.

The smallest of Big Bend's bats is the **Western Pipistrelle,** common along the Rio Grande floodplain. The largest is the huge **Western Mastiff Bat**, which is never abundant, but I have seen it often near the river during spring and fall. Other species of bats recorded in the park include the **Yuma, Cave, Fringed, Long-legged, California,** and **Small-footed** myotis; **Big Brown Bat, Red Bat, Hoary Bat, Townsend's Big-eared Bat, Pallid Bat; Brazilian Free-tailed, Pocketed,** and **Big Free-tailed** bats; **Ghost-faced** and **Long-nosed** bats. The last species, which roosts in a cave high on the north side of Emory Peak, has not been found anywhere else in the United States.

The smallest of Big Bend's mammals is the **Desert Shrew.** This little predator is extremely shy and has been recorded from the floodplain to the top of the Chisos Mountains.

Daytime mammals usually are more conspicuous than those that prefer the nighttime. Watch for the **Rock Squirrel** on the rock bridges in Green Gulch, but you may also find it near the river or near the South Rim. The **Texas Antelope Squirrel** is wide-ranging, too. This little squirrel looks very much like a chipmunk and is often called that, but it lacks the white face stripe of the chipmunk. The Texas Antelope Squirrel is one of the few ground squirrels that does not hibernate in winter. The two species of ground squirrels found only in the lowlands of the park do hibernate. The **Mexican Ground Squirrel** is rare in the park, but you can usually find it in summer at Rio Grande Village. A walk through the campground, from April through September, will almost always turn up at least one of these Mexican mammals. The fourth Big Bend ground squirrel is the **Spotted Ground Squirrel**. It can be found up to about 4,000 feet elevation but is not common. Its spots are scattered rather than arranged in rows, as they are on the former species.

The only other mammals you are likely to see during the daytime are rabbits, represented by three species: the **Black-tailed Jack Rabbit**, the **Eastern Cottontail** in the mountains, and the **Desert Cottontail** below the woodlands.

8. Birds

IT probably will come as a surprise to find out that more kinds of birds have been recorded in Big Bend National Park than in any other National Park Service area. More than 395 species have been reported, of which only about 35 are considered hypothetical, that is, species not authenticated by a specimen or sightings by two or more individuals or parties. The official park checklist, which is revised every two or three years, categorizes all of the birds into four classes: Summer, After Breeding, Winter, and Migrant. The July, 1971, list included 107 species in the summer listing—those which are known to breed within the park. Seventy-one species occur as post-nesting visitors in summer, and 169 are winter birds—"permanent residents and those which may arrive as early as September, remain all winter, and may stay as late as April" (Wauer 1973, p. 54). Migrants make up the largest group. Altogether, 252 species have been recorded as migrating through the park in spring and/or fall. As can be realized by totaling these numbers, there is considerable duplication among the four categories.

The birder who wants to find the greatest number of the park's birds should plan his visit during the last two weeks of April and the first week of May, when the summering birds have arrived on their nesting grounds and the greatest concentration of migrants can be found. If you visit all of the various habitats in a day or two, you may sight 100 to 120 bird species. The following is a suggested route for your observations.

Start at Rio Grande Village. Check the fields northwest of the store, the cottonwood grove at the end of the road running west from the store, and the silt pond that lies beyond the cottonwood grove. Then head for the nature trail and campground. This area can be excellent during migration. If time allows, visit the area of Boquillas Crossing and the mesquite-cactus field just west of Boquillas Canyon.

After covering this lowland area, head for the Chisos Basin. En route, stop for a few minutes at Dugout and check along Green Gulch near the upper and lower water barrels. In the Basin, start with the Window Trail. Hike down the trail from the campground to the lowest edge of the oaks, and then return up the trail to a point where Oak Creek drainage passes near the trail just below the sewage lagoons. From there, follow the wash up the canyon past the lagoons to where a roadway from the campground enters the drainage at a chlorination station. The oak tree above the large flat tank is used as a nesting tree by **Elf Owls**. Follow the road to the campground and return to your vehicle.

The high country is next. If you can stay overnight at Boot Springs, take the Boot Canyon Trail through Juniper Flat, past Boulder Meadow, over Pinnacle Pass, and down into Boot Canyon. If you cannot camp overnight at Boot Springs, take the South Rim Trail from the Basin. Laguna Meadow is 3.5 miles along the trail, and this area can produce almost as many migrants as Boot Canyon. Continue past the meadow to the side trail to Boot Canyon, and return to the Basin via the Boot Springs Trail. At Boot Springs, be sure to walk up the canyon for about half a mile.

Most of the world's finest birding places feature a few specialties to go along with its regulars, and Big Bend National Park is no exception. In fact, birders really get their share of specialties here, including a few species that are not known elsewhere in the United States. Anyone boasting the addition of the **Colima Warbler** and **Lucifer Hummingbird** to his list must have visited Big Bend National Park in spring or summer.

The Colima Warbler is the most famous of the park's birds. This little gray and yellow warbler is known nowhere else in the United States. It nests in Boot Canyon, the adjacent high, cool canyons in the Chisos Mountains and south into Mexico's inaccessible mountains. Even in the Chisos, however, the birder must expend some energy to see it. Boot Canyon is the most reliable locality to find the Colima, although it also nests at Laguna Meadow most summers.

The Lucifer Hummingbird is another of the park's specialties. Although it has been recorded elsewhere along the Mexican border, Big Bend National Park is the only place in the United States where this bird occurs regularly. In fact, throughout most of the summer it is one of the park's most common hummers. It usually can be found near blooming Century Plants. And, in summer, look for it among the bright red flowers of the Mountain Sage within the mountain wood-lands.

The **Varied Bunting** usually can be found in the park with little problem during late spring and summer. They nest in the brushy grasslands and can be sighted at the Old Ranch, Government Spring, and along the Window Trail just below the lagoons.

The **Flammulated Owl** is difficult to find anywhere. However, during May, June, and early July you can usually find one just beyond the cabin in Boot Canyon. The low, single note, "oo," can be heard all summer. At dusk, sit on a rock along the trail where it crosses the drainage; the owl will appear just as dark arrives.

The **Black-chinned Sparrow** can be found throughout the year, although it is easiest to find in summer near the sewage lagoons in the lower basin and in the chaparral growth along the lower half of the South Rim Trail; this bird is most numerous along the northern edge of Laguna Meadow.

A visit in summer is not complete without birding the lowlands. Two readily accessible areas are along the Rio Grande at Rio Grande Village and the area between Castolon and Santa Elena Canyon. Some of the most common nesting birds of these areas include the **White-winged Dove** and **Mourning Dove, Yellow-billed Cuckoo, Roadrun-ner, Lesser Nighthawk, Black-chinned Hummingbird, Ladder-backed Woodpecker, Verdin, Mockingbird, Black-tailed Gnat-catcher, Bell's Vireo, Yellow-breasted Chat, Orchard Oriole, Brown-headed Cowbird, Summer Tanager, Blue Grosbeak,** and **Painted Bunting.**

There are several other lowland birds that you may want to see and can find with the proper directions. **Peregrines** have nested within the larger canyons during recent years. Watch for these magnificent birds along the trails in Boquillas and Santa Elena canyons. In 1971, a pair of Peregrines nested just inside Santa Elena Canyon, on the Mexi-can side.

Vermilion Flycatchers are most numerous within and adjacent to Rio Grande Village and Cottonwood campgrounds. As many as eight or ten of these beautiful birds can usually be found in summer. Rio Grande Village Campground is also the site where the **Black-vented Oriole** appeared during the summers of 1969 and 1970. Although the Black-vented Oriole has not been seen in the United States before or

Elephant Tusk and Fresno Creek from the South Rim.

Punta de la Sierra from the grassy edge of the South Rim.

Sunset at the South Rim.

Roadrunners are fairly common within the Big Bend lowlands. Their strange behavior includes the male's enticement of favors from the female by giving her lizards. Photo by Hopkins.

since, the **Hooded Oriole** nests there every summer. And in recent years, **Bronzed Cowbirds** have begun to summer in the campgrounds as well. Careful study should be made of these social parasites. It is likely that nesting Orioles will decrease with the presence of the Bronzed Cowbird, since the Cowbird discards Oriole eggs from their nests and lays her own eggs there.

Peregrine Falcons still inhabit the canyons and mountains of the Big Bend Country. Their presence attests to the unpolluted environment that is preserved within the park area. CDRI photo.

As the summer wanes, many of the park's breeding birds begin to move about from place to place. Floodplain and desert birds can often be found in the woodlands, and woodland birds can sometimes be found on the floodplain. During this season, it is not too unlikely to find **Mississippi Kites** and **Zone-tailed Hawks** along the river at Rio Grande Village and near Castolon.

This is the time of the year, too, when breeding birds from elsewhere may reach the park. Watch around the ponds at Rio Grande Village for **Louisiana Herons** and **Black-crowned Night Herons** and **Yellow-crowned Night Herons**. A number of puddle ducks put in their appearance, and the **Mexican Duck** may be seen along the river. A lucky birder may discover a **Least Grebe** or **Green Kingfisher** on the ponds.

In recent years, the **Groove-billed Ani** has become a regular visitor to the heavier areas of vegetation along the floodplain. Look for it in August and September along the Rio Grande Village Nature Trail.

The mountains can also produce some interesting post-nesting visitors. **Hummingbirds** are attracted to Mountain Sage flowers and it is possible, in late July and early August, to find as many as eleven species of hummers: **Lucifer, Ruby-throated, Black-chinned, Broad-tailed, Rufous, Allen's, Calliope, Rivoli's, Blue-throated, White-eared,** and **Broad-billed.**

Warblers begin to move into the mountain canyons during the first week of August, and a visit to Boot Canyon can produce the **Black-and-white, Orange-crowned, Nashville, Virginia's, Colima, Yellow, Audubon's, Black-throated Gray, Townsend's, Black-throated Green, Hermit, Grace's,** and **Wilson's.**

The discovery of an **Aztec Thrush** in Boot Canyon on August 21, 1977, is almost unbelievable. David Wolf and friends first observed and photographed this bird, previously endemic to the Mexican highlands, and it was found again four days later. It is difficult to find this bird in suitable habitat in Mexico; therefore, its presence so far out of range in the United States is even more remarkable.

Big Bend's wintering birds are seldom spectacular. However, a number of species are of interest to birders. High-mountain birds are few and far between, and the majority of the mountain species can be found along the Window and Lost Mine trails.

Band-tailed Pigeons can usually be seen from along the terminal ridge of the Lost Mine Trail. Look into the Ponderosa Pine area in the canyon to the east of the trail. From there, too, you can usually see **White-throated Swifts, Golden Eagles, Western Bluebirds, Townsend's Solitaire, Golden-crowned Kinglets, Hutton's Vireos,** and **Juncos.** Sometimes you can also find **Williamson's Sapsuckers, Red-breasted Nuthatches, Cassin's Finches,** and **Red Crossbills.**

The Window Trail, just above and below the sewage lagoons, usually produces a handful of wintering species as well. Watch there for the **White-winged Dove, Crissal Thrasher, Phainopepla,** and **Black-chinned Sparrow.**

Once again, Rio Grande Village and the floodplain between Castolon and Santa Elena Canyon are the best places for lowland birding in winter. During warm winters, with some searching you can often find the **Ash-throated Flycatcher** and the **Dusky Flycatcher.** The **Crissal Thrasher** can be found on the mesquite flats across the roadway from the Santa Elena Canyon picnic sites and on the flat near Boquillas Canyon. Watch there, too, for the **Sage Thrasher** and **Curve-billed Thrasher.**

The White-winged Dove has been limited to only a small part of its former range through reduction of suitable habitat. It is still common within Big Bend National Park. Photo by Porter.

Some of the most exciting winter birding will result from walks through some of the old, weedy fields below Castolon and along Alamo Creek. You can usually find the **Green-tailed Towhee** and **Savannah, Vesper, Clay-colored, Brewer's, White-crowned,** and **Lincoln's** sparrows with little trouble. More time and good luck may turn up the **Grasshopper, Baird's, Cassin's, Field, White-throated,** and **Swamp** sparrows.

9. Reptiles and Amphibians

THE excitement generated by reptiles and amphibians is too often a negative excitement, for man seems far more interested in hair-raising stories than in fact. There probably are more old wives' tales about snakes, lizards, and toads than any other group of animals. Who has not heard that "hoop-snakes" put their tails in their mouths and roll down hills, or that snakes have the ability to hypnotize their prey? Some cowboys still spread horsehair ropes around their bedrolls at night to keep snakes away. And how many people still believe that toads cause warts? All false but fascinating!

The many true stories about reptiles and amphibians are just as amazing. In fact, herpetology, the scientific study of these animals, has become popular in many colleges and universities throughout the United States, particularly in the Southwest. It is in the warmer areas of North America that the majority of America's 300 kinds of reptiles and many of the 700 kinds of amphibians are found.

Few places in the Southwest have more snakes and lizards than Big Bend National Park. Yet, surprisingly enough, the study of the reptiles and amphibians there was neglected for many years. Until the 1940's, herpetological research in the Big Bend area was only a by-product of more intense studies in other fields. Karl P. Schmidt and T. F. Smith published the first comprehensive summary of Big Bend reptiles and amphibians in 1944. This annotated listing still constitutes the most complete published summary for the park area, although William Milstead and William Degenhardt did considerable herpetological research in the park during the 1950's and 1960's.

Roger Conant, who in 1958 completed his well-known *A Field Guide to Reptiles and Amphibians of Eastern North America*, took as his western boundary the 100th meridian. This north-south line extends from central Texas through the middle of the Dakotas north to western Manitoba and Keewatin, Canada. Not until 1966 did Robert C. Stebbins complete *A Field Guide to Western Reptiles and Amphi-*

bians, which included all of the western states of Canada and the United States east to Saskatchewan, Montana, Wyoming, Colorado, and New Mexico. Sadly, it did not cover the whole of the Trans-Pecos and the western portions of Oklahoma, Kansas, Nebraska, South and North Dakota, Manitoba, and Keewatin. Although the ranges of most species overlap enough to cover the neglected areas, this was not true for a great many forms in the western half of Texas. Not until 1975, with the publication of Roger Conant's revised *A Field Guide to Reptiles and Amphibians of Eastern and Central North America*, was the gap filled. That volume now includes all fifty-five reptiles—four turtles, twenty-one lizards and thirty snakes—and ten amphibians known in Big Bend National Park.

With such an assortment, you might assume that snakes and lizards are commonplace in the area and that you would have to go out of your way to avoid them. On the contrary, you could travel all of the roads and hike all of the trails without seeing a single snake and probably sighting only a handful of lizards. Although both are present throughout the area, they are seldom active during the heat of a summer day and during the colder months of winter. Being cold-blooded, reptiles and amphibians cannot survive long in cold weather or direct desert heat and must seek shelter.

On occasion, a frog, turtle, or small lizard may be active on warmer days in winter. The **Rio Grande Leopard Frog** (*Rana berlandieri*) lives along the Rio Grande and at most of the park's permanent ponds and springs. Although you may not see this slim, green, spotted frog, you will surely hear its strange assortment of grunts and low chuckles in these areas.

By March, warm evenings along the waterways and at waterholes feature a chorus of amphibian songs. Most common is the high-pitched trill, in C or C minor, of the **Red-spotted Toad** (*Bufo punctatus*), which may be found at Hot Springs along Tornillo Creek or on Terlingua Creek near Santa Elena Canyon. A wide-ranging species, it also occurs up to elevations of about 5,500 feet in the Chisos woodlands.

Toads are most often found on park roads following summer rainstorms. **Woodhouse's Toad** (*B. woodhousei*) is rare, restricted almost entirely to the river floodplain and adjacent washes. The **Western Green Toad** (*B. debilis insidior*) occurs throughout the desert lowlands and up into the Chisos foothills. And the **Texas Toad** (*B. speciosus*) is fairly common on the floodplain but has been found within the shrub desert on a few occasions.

Two spadefoot toads reside within Big Bend Park's shrub desert as well. The common species is **Couch's Spadefoot** (*Scaphiopus couchi*), but the **Western Spadefoot** (*S. hammondi*) also has been reported. Spadefoots have a single hard "spade" on the underside of each foot, which they use to dig backward into the earth. They are able to bury themselves in a cool, protective burrow where they secrete a gelatinous coat about themselves to retain their body moisture. They may spend the majority of their lives underground, venturing out of their hiding places after summer rainstorms to find pools of water from which they sing to attract a mate so that they can breed before again seeking shelter underground.

The **Canyon Treefrog** (*Hyla arenicolor*) and **Cliff Frog** (*Syrrhophus marnocki*) occur in the mountainous parts of the park. The Canyon Treefrog is fairly common at water areas within the upper canyons, where its loud call, like that of a bleating kid goat, may be heard throughout the night. The Cliff Frog lives among the rocky cliffs

The Canyon Treefrog is found in the moist, rocky canyons in the higher elevations of the Chisos Mountains. Photo by Wauer.

and talus slopes and occasionally ventures onto the roadways in Green Gulch and the Chisos Basin. This and the **Great Plains Narrow-mouthed Toad** (*Gastrophryne olivacea*) are the smallest of Big Bend's amphibians, seldom more than one and a half inches in length. Narrow-mouthed toads occur at water areas throughout the lowlands and are easily detected by their characteristic buzzing call, which is more like the sound of an angry bee than an amphibian.

Three of Big Bend's four turtle species reside at water areas. The most widespread is the **Yellow Mud Turtle** (*Kinosternon flavescens*), which is common along the Rio Grande and its tributaries but also breeds in rain-filled earthen tanks up to the Chisos woodlands. The **Texas Spiny Softshell** (*Trionyx spiniferus emoryi*) is restricted to permanent waters of the Rio Grande and adjacent ponds. This is the largest of Big Bend's turtles; a female may reach more than fourteen inches in length. Often in summer they can be found basking in the sun at pond edges at Rio Grande Village. There, too, may be found the **Big Bend Turtle** (*Chrysemys scripta gaigeae*) resting atop a log or rock partially submerged in water. This species can be identified by the red patch on the side of its head.

The **Desert Box Turtle** (*Terrapene ornata luteola*) is Big Bend's only dry land turtle. Since they are uncommon, the discovery of one of these reptiles sauntering across the desert flat is an exciting find indeed. In recent years the **Texas Tortoise** (*Gopherus berlandieri*) has been found within the Chisos Basin on a couple of occasions. Since the woodlands of the Chisos Mountains are not only the improper habitat but also a considerable distance from its natural range in East Texas, it is believed that the tortoises were released there by thoughtless visitors. Park rangers have found transportation for them back to their proper home. Turtles are easily captured; they become a unique plaything for a few days and are then discarded when they are no longer a novelty. Such carelessness undoubtedly has reduced the already low population of some of the Southwest's most unusual reptiles and amphibians.

Lizards

Lizards usually are more easily observed than any of the other forms of herptiles. Except for geckos, all are active during the daylight hours. The **Texas Banded Gecko** (*Coleonyx brevis*) is fairly common from the floodplain up into the Chisos Mountains. These fat-tailed little lizards can often be found walking across the roads at night.

Until the summer of 1972, the **Big Bend Gecko** (*Coleonyx reticulatus*) was known to science from less than half a dozen specimens taken from northeast of the park in the vicinity of the Black Gap Wildlife Management Area. When several more of these lizards were discovered in 1972, including one inside the park, the species was considered to be valid. Since then it has been surprisingly common during the summer rainy season.

More recently, a third gecko was discovered within the park. The **Mediterranean Gecko** (*Hemidactylus t. turcicus*) is exotic to North America, but has been known to be in Texas for more than two decades. In July 1972, George (Stoney) Burdick and I found several individuals in buildings at Boquillas, Coahuila, Mexico, just across the river from Rio Grande Village. Since then the Mediterranean Gecko has found its way to Rio Grande Village, where it can often be found on buildings near lights. It will be interesting to watch its progress westward along the Rio Grande.

Most lizards are quite shy by nature, and so to observe them, you must approach slowly or they will run away and hide. Skinks probably are the most secretive. They conceal themselves under leaves and other debris so well that they are seldom seen unless you are looking for them. Usually they can be detected by their movement under dry leaves, and a patient wait until they reappear is necessary. Watch for the **Great Plains Skink** (*Eumeces obsoletus*) along the Rio Grande Village Nature Trail and similar places of heavy vegetation along the floodplain and up into the Chisos Mountains. The **Short-lined Skink** (*E. tetragrammus brevilineatus*) prefers the cooler canyons of the mountains but occasionally is seen in moist places such as Dugout in the lowlands.

The most commonly seen lizard of Big Bend's shrub desert environment is the **Long-nosed Southwestern Earless Lizard** (*Holbrookia texana scitula*). This very fast lizard usually is seen running along the roadway or crossing in front of your vehicle. Adult males are extremely colorful, green overall with two black-on-blue chevrons on their sides just above the back legs. At night they burrow into gravel or sand or, occasionally, may be found sleeping on park roadways.

The Collared Lizard , a swift predator that runs down its prey, is a resident of the rocky slopes of the lower Chisos Mountains. Photo by Wauer.

The **Collared Lizard** (*Crotaphytus collaris*) and **Leopard Lizard** (*C. w. wislizenii*) are large, swift-running lizards. These creatures may be as much as fourteen inches from nose to tail tip and are able to prey upon smaller lizards and snakes. They prefer open, sandy soils and are rather uncommon within the Big Bend Park area.

Four kinds of spiny lizards are known to occur within the park. The **Crevice Spiny Lizard** (*Sceloporus p. poinsetti*) and **Big Bend Canyon Lizard** (*S. merriami annulatus*) are wide-ranging species occurring from the Rio Grande floodplain to the upper canyons of the Chisos Mountains. Both live in rocky washes and cliffs and may be locally common. The Big Bend Canyon Lizard is of special interest because it occurs only within the southern portion of the Big Bend east to Terrell and Val Verde counties in the United States and in northern Mexico adjacent to the Rio Grande.

The **Southern Prairie Lizard** (*S. undulatus consobrinus*) prefers yucca and shrub desert areas and the wooded parts of the lower mountains. The **Twin-spotted Spiny Lizard** (*S. magister bimaculosus*) is the least common member of this group of lizards and resides in mesquite thickets along the river and rarely in desert washes to about 3,500 feet.

Big Bend Park has four whiptails as well. The most widespread of these is the **Marbled Whiptail** (*Cnemidophorus tigris marmoratus*), which is a common ground dweller on the river floodplain and desert flats and less so in the Chisos foothills up to 4,500 feet. The **Checkered Whiptail** (*C. tesselatus*) prefers the river canyons, where it hides among the reeds. The **Seven-striped Whiptail** (*C. inornatus heptagrammus*) resides on the desert flats and low foothills and is often associated with Lechuguilla and yuccas. The **Rusty-rumped Whiptail** (*C. scalaris septemvittatus*) prefers the mountain foothills and may be locally common from 3,000 to 7,000 feet elevation.

Two horned lizards have been found within the park, but only one, the **Round-tailed Horned Lizard** (*Phrynosoma modestum*), occurs regularly on the desert flats and lower foothills. Considerable variation in the color has been noticed in this species; those of the Chisos foothills are often quite pink, while those from the lower clay flats are much lighter in color. The **Texas Horned Lizard** (*P. cornutum*) is rare within the park, and until the summer of 1969 when several were found on upper Tornillo Flat, its presence within the area had not been definitely authenticated.

The **Desert Side-blotched Lizard** (*Uta stansburiana stejnegeri*) is a wide-ranging species that occurs uncommonly from the floodplain of the Rio Grande up into the lower foothills of the Chisos Mountains. It may be the only lizard seen during early spring when temperatures do not yet allow larger lizards to be active. A closely related species is the **Big Bend Tree Lizard** (*Urosaurus ornatus schmidti*). Probably more common than sightings indicate, it is a very shy species that lives on trees and cliffs from the upper desert washes to the canyons of the mountains. In Pine Canyon it is found on Ponderosa Pines.

Only one of Big Bend's lizards resides just in the upper parts of the mountains, the **Texas Alligator Lizard** (*Gerrhonotus liocephalus infernalis*). It looks more like a salamander than a lizard and prefers the cooler woodlands of the park. Although rare in spring and early summer, it becomes fairly common after the summer rainy season begins.

Snakes

Snakes comprise the largest group of Big Bend's herptiles. The **Central Texas Whipsnake** (*Masticophis taeniatus ornatus*), **Bullsnake** (*Pituophis melanoleucus sayi*), **Regal Ringneck Snake** (*Diadophis punctatus regalis*), and **Black-tailed Rattlesnake** (*Crotalus m. molossus*) have been reported for all elevations. The whipsnakes and bullsnakes are diurnal in habits and so usually are seen more than those species active mainly at night. In fact, the **Western Coachwhip** (*Masticophis flagellum testaceus*), which is common in the shrub desert and lower foothills, is one of the park's most conspicuous snakes. Because of its red color and swiftness, it is often called the "red racer," although it is not a true racer. However, a pink snake crossing the desert roadway in front of your vehicle does demand an explanation!

The **Regal Ringneck Snake** (*Diadophis punctatus regalis*) is fairly common within the Chisos foothills and cool canyons of the highlands but is rare on the river floodplain. This colorful species is sometimes called the "thimble snake" because of its habit of twisting its brilliant orange-red tail into a tight "thimble" or spiral when alarmed. The waving, brightly colored tail may attract a predator's attention away from more vulnerable parts of the body.

Early in spring, before ground temperatures become warm enough for larger snakes to appear, patch-nosed snakes may be seen during the late afternoons and evenings. The **Big Bend Patch-nosed Snake** (*Salvadora deserticola*) occurs throughout the lowlands up into the Chisos foothills, and the **Mountain Patch-nosed Snake** (*S. g. grahamiae*) resides above 3,500 feet.

Two blind or worm snakes have been reported for Big Bend National Park. Both are wide-ranging species occurring from the river floodplain up into the pinyon-juniper woodland. The **Trans-Pecos Blind Snake** (*Leptotyphlops humilis segregus*) is the more common of the two, but the **New Mexico Blind Snake** (*L. dulcis dissectus*) has been found on a number of occasions. Both species are most active following summer rainstorms.

The **Trans-Pecos Ground Snake** (*Sonora semiannulata blanchardi*) and **Spotted Night Snake** (*Hypsiglena torquata ochrorhyncha*) are two other small nocturnal species. Sonora ranges from the shrub desert to the Chisos Basin and may have one of three color phases.

Unicolor olive to gray is most common, but unicolor orange and ringed phases do occur. The night snake is a fairly common species of the desert and lower Chisos foothills.

Tantillas, or black-headed snakes, are also small nocturnal species. Two, or possibly three, of these are found within the park. The most widespread of the group is the **Mexican Black-headed Snake** (*Tantilla atriceps*), which occurs from the upper desert to the Chisos Basin. The **Black-hooded Snake** (*T. rubra cucullata*) has been found in the Chisos Mountains on several occasions. Sherman M. Minton, Jr., first discovered it in the Del Norte Mountains just west of Alpine, Texas, on July 1, 1955. The Black-hooded Snake's entire known range extends only from the Chisos Mountains north to the southern edge of the Davis Mountains; it has not been found elsewhere. About the same time, a similar species was described from the Devils River area and is referred to as the **Devils River Black-headed Snake** (*T. rubra diabola*).

Some extremely rare snakes occur within Big Bend Park. The **Texas Lyre Snake** (*Trimorphodon biscutatus vilkinsoni*) is one of those that has been reported on only a few occasions in the desert and Chisos Basin. A Mexican species, it occurs within the United States only from the Big Bend west to southern New Mexico. Another hard-to-find snake is the **Gray-banded Kingsnake** (*Lampropeltis mexicana alterna*). A mountain-dwelling species, it is restricted to the Chisos, Davis, and Sierra Vieja mountains in the United States south to San Luis Potosí in Mexico.

Two other kingsnakes occur within the Chisos Mountains: the **Desert Kingsnake** (*L. getulus splendida*) and **Mexican Milk Snake** (*L. triangulum annulata*). The former species has been found at Castolon and in the Chisos foothills, while the latter species has been found only in the Chisos Basin.

The **Western Hook-nosed Snake** (*Gyalopion canum*) is another mountain species that has been considered quite rare. In recent years, however, it has been found regularly in the moist canyons, although it was not known in the park before 1944.

The **Texas Glossy Snake** (*Arizona elegans arenicola*) and **Texas Long-nosed Snake** (*Rhinocheilus lecontei tessellatus*) are fairly common species on creosote bush flats of the lowland desert and Chisos foothills.

Three rat snakes are known to occur within Big Bend Park. One of

The Gray-banded Kingsnake is another of the Big Bend specialties. This species has a wide assortment of color patterns and is truly one of our most beautiful reptiles. Photo by Porter.

these, the **Trans-Pecos Rat Snake** (*Elaphe subocularis*), is restricted to a range from the Big Bend and Guadalupe mountains to southern New Mexico. In recent years its numbers seem to have increased in the park, although it is rarely found elsewhere. **Baird's Rat Snake** (*E. obsoleta bairdi*) is a mountain species, and the **Great Plains Rat Snake** (*E. guttata emoryi*) is a snake of the lower Chihuahuan Desert. Both are uncommon in occurrence.

Three of Big Bend's snakes are restricted to a water environment. The **Blotched Water Snake** (*Natrix erythrogaster transversa*), found only along the Rio Grande and adjacent ponds, has become quite rare in recent years. Two garter snakes are fairly common, however. The **Checkered Garter Snake** (*Thamnophis m. marcianus*) has been found only in the lowland waterways, while the **Western Black-necked Garter Snake** (*T. c. cyrtopsis*) has a much wider range from the lower foothills up to the highlands of the Chisos Mountains. This is the species that is common in summer along Boot Canyon.

Six poisonous snakes have been reported for Big Bend National Park. The **Prairie Rattlesnake** (*Crotalus v. viridis*) has not been found in the park for several years; it was most likely extirpated before the

The Black-tailed Rattlesnake occurs from the highest peaks to the lowest portion of the Big Bend Country. Photo by Wauer.

establishment of the park, when the grasslands were seriously depleted. The **Black-tailed Rattlesnake** is the most widespread rattler, as it has been recorded for the river floodplain up into the highest mountains. Although rarely seen in the lowlands, it is the common rattler of the Chisos woodlands. The common desert rattler is the **Western Diamondback Rattlesnake** (*C. atrox*), and the **Mojave Rattlesnake** (*C. s. scutulatus*) is uncommon within the same range. Degenhardt believes that the Mojave Rattlesnake, too, has increased in recent years. The **Mottled Rock Rattlesnake** (*C. l. lepidus*) is another mountain species that occasionally is found about rocky places from the lower foothills to Emory Peak. Pink and green phases of this snake occur regularly.

The sixth poisonous snake of Big Bend Park is the **Trans-Pecos Copperhead** (*Agkistrodon contortrix pictigaster*). Although the type specimen was taken in Green Gulch at 5,200 feet elevation, the snake is more common at patches of cane along the Rio Grande. It has been found from the banks of the Rio Grande to the Davis Mountains and east to Sanderson, Texas.

10. Fish

AT only a few places within Big Bend National Park will the environment support fish. The Rio Grande and its two tributaries, Tornillo and Terlingua creeks, are virtually the only inhabited locations. About three dozen species of fish have been recorded, but the average fisherman seldom sees more than two or three. Most fishermen are after the tasty catfish found there—the **Blue, Channel,** and **Flathead.** The Blue and Flathead are the most common and a favored food fish. Occasionally, a **Longnose Gar** is caught. This predatory fish with a long, pointed snout and sharp teeth may be four feet in length. **Gizzard Shad** frequent quiet waters of the Rio Grande, and the **Blue Sucker** prefers swift currents. Other Rio Grande fish large enough for a fisherman's hook include **Smallmouth Buffalo, River Carpsucker, Carp,** and **Freshwater Drum.** In 1954, an **American Eel** was taken from the Rio Grande near Castolon. It is doubtful that this species will ever again be found in the park because Amistad and Falcon dams stop upstream migration of these fish, which breed in the ocean.

Most of the park's native fish are of minnow size. Three of these were listed as rare, restricted, and/or threatened by Robert Rush Miller in 1963: **Mexican Stoneroller** is known in the United States only from the park area and Rucker Canyon in Arizona's Chiricahua Mountains; **Chihuahua Shiner** inhabits the United States only in the park; and **Big Bend Gambusia** is restricted to a small pond at Rio Grande Village. In fact, this last species covers the smallest geographic range of any known vertebrate.

Big Bend Gambusia was first found at Boquillas Spring in 1928 and described by Carl L. Hubbs the following year. That spring dried up, however, and until 1954, when another population was discovered near Rio Grande Village, the species was considered extinct. The second population was threatened by development for an expanding campground, as well as by competition from other fish, until a pond especially for the species was constructed on the site (Hubbs and Brod-

The confluence of the Rio Grande and Tornillo Creek is marked by the historic site of Hot Springs, a popular resort during the 1930's. Photo by Wauer.

rick 1963). The park continued to have difficulty protecting this endemic fish in spite of its isolated locality in the park. Thoughtless fishermen had made a practice of dumping unused live bait into the ponds at Rio Grande Village. "Gambusia Pond" was no exception, despite signs at each corner of the pond asking people not to dump fish there. But when I discovered that this pond was populated with **Green Sunfish** and **Mosquitofish**, I knew we had to spend the considerable time and money necessary to save this endangered species.

First, an adjacent pond was dried up and all of the fish there (Mosquitofish, **Goldfish**, **Bluegill**, and Green Sunfish) were eliminated. Water was later replaced and allowed to stand for three weeks so that a natural supply of food developed. Second, Roger Siglin and I collected more than 250 Big Bend Gambusias from the main pond. About 150 were deposited in the adjacent pond, and we took the rest of the collection to an aquarium at park headquarters. "Gambusia Pond" was then dried up and all of the fish in that pond were eliminated. Water was added and allowed to stand for about one month before all of the aquarium fish were reintroduced. The population increased noticeably within a few weeks.

Although the Big Bend Gambusias were safe for the time being, there was no guarantee that other fish would not soon be dumped into the pond again. Because the previous signs had not been successful, I prepared a text for a new sign that was installed soon after the reintroduction. It reads, "Fish So Fragile—This pond contains the world's population of Gambusia gaigei. These minnow-sized fish have lived here since Mastodons. Unique and fragile, they survive only because man wants to make it so." At this writing, ten years later, no other fish have been found in the Big Bend Gambusia Pond.

The 1973 Endangered Species Act provided greater protection for a variety of vertebrates, including the Big Bend Gambusia. The National Park Service had given full protection to this endangered fish but had done little to restore its environment to the conditions existing before Rio Grande Village Campground was constructed. And so Clark Hubbs, Jim Johnson (Fish and Wildlife Service endangered species biologist), and I prepared a plan for the management of this unique species. The plan aims at the restoration of a spring flow near Rio Grande Village where Big Bend Gambusia will be permitted to survive in a habitat as similar as possible to that existing before the development of Rio Grande Village.

Clark Hubbs of the University of Texas has been interested in fish of the Big Bend Country for many years. It was because of his interest and insistence that the Big Bend Gambusia was saved in the beginning. But his interest did not stop there. He and I took monthly samplings of fish along the lower end of Tornillo Creek for three years to find out if a seasonal change of fish fauna occurred there. We found that the creek served as a breeding and nursery area for several Rio Grande fish, yet none of the fish appeared to be permanent residents. The **Mexican Tetra, Redhorse** and **Chihuahua** shiners, **Mexican Stoneroller, Plains Killifish,** and Mosquitofish used lower Tornillo Creek for breeding and rearing young. Possibly, the creek environment is necessary for the survival of those species in the Big Bend area. Most of the fish species used the creek only for a nursery, but young were also common in the Rio Grande. Shiners seem to occupy the creek in warm months but were sparse there in cold months. The Mexican Stoneroller and Plains Killifish were common in the creek during cool months and sparse in warmer periods.

The following is a complete list of the fish that have been recorded in Big Bend National Park and immediate vicinity.

Longnose Gar	*Lepisosteus osseus* (Linnaeus)
Gizzard Shad	*Dorosoma cepedianum* (LeSueur)
Mexican Tetra	*Astyanax mexicanus* (Filippi)
Mexican Stoneroller	*Campostoma ornatum* (Girard)
Carp	*Cyprinus carpio* (Linnaeus)
Goldfish	*Carassius auratus* (Girard)
Roundnose Minnow	*Dionda episcopa* (Girard)
Speckled Chub	*Hybopsis aestivalis* (Girard)
Tamaulipas Shiner	*Notropis braytoni* (Jordan and Evermann)
Chihuahua Shiner	*Notropis chihuahua* (Woolman)
Rio Grande Shiner	*Notropis jemenzanus* (Cope)
Red Shiner	*Notropis lutrensis* (Baird and Girard)
Bluntnose Shiner	*Notropis simus* (Cope)
Flathead Minnow	*Pimephales promelas* (Rafinesque)
Longnose Dace	*Rhinichthys cataractae* (Valenciennes)
River Carpsucker	*Carpiodes carpio* (Rafinesque)
Smallmouth Buffalo	*Ictiobus bubalus* (Rafinesque)
Blue Sucker	*Cycleptus elongatus* (LeSueur)
Gray Redhorse	*Moxostoma congestum* (Baird and Girard)
Blue Catfish	*Ictalurus furcatus* (LeSueur)
Channel Catfish	*Ictalurus pinctatus* (Rafinesque)
Flathead Catfish	*Pylodictis olivaris* (Rafinesque)
American Eel	*Anguilla rostrata* (LeSueur)
Plains Killifish	*Fundulus kansae* (Garman)
Mosquitofish	*Gambusia affinis* (Baird and Girard)
Big Bend Gambusia	*Gambusia gaigei* (Hubbs)
Warmouth	*Chaenobryttus gulosus* (Curvier)
Green Sunfish	*Chaenobryttus cyanellus* (Rafinesque)
Bluegill	*Lepomis macrochirius* (Rafinesque)
Longear Sunfish	*Lepomis megalotis* (Rafinesque)
Redear Sunfish	*Lepomis microlophus* (Gunther)
Largemouth Bass	*Micropterus salmoides* (Lacopide)
Freshwater Drum	*Aplodinotus grunniens* (Rafinesque)
Rio Grande Perch	*Chichlasoma cyanoguttatum* (Baird and Girard)
Tidewater Silverside	*Menidia beryllina* (Cope)

11. Insects and Other Invertebrates

STRANGELY enough, the desert is very full of life. Although some of the larger animals, especially mammals, are seen only occasionally, thousands of smaller creatures can be found with a little searching. In the desert, as elsewhere, many smaller animals may be required to feed only one predator. Little creatures often feed upon even smaller ones. The chain is like a huge pyramid, supported on the bottom by the multitudes of tiny creatures, with the higher forms of life on top.

The great array of life at the bottom of the pyramid of life is made up of insects and other invertebrates. Because they are cold-blooded, they are most active during the warm parts of the year and are rare in winter. Particularly when the summer rains begin, you cannot travel far in the desert without seeing at least a few invertebrates. The rather fat and long segmented "worms" found crawling across the desert roadways are **Millipedes**. Big Bend's millipede is *Orthoporus ornatus*, a scavenger that feeds primarily upon decaying plant materials. The millipede is not as harmful as it first appears, although when disturbed it usually rolls into a tight circle and emits brown fluid that smells like cyanide through openings along the sides of its body. The ejected fluid is harmless to humans but can actually kill insects placed in the same jar. The bodies of many dead millipedes can often be found on the desert after summer storms. Their dried and bleached skeletons look like a series of small white rings.

The **Giant Desert Centipede** (*Scolopendra heros*) is even more formidable in appearance. This creature does not have as many legs as the millipede, but it is faster and preys upon insects, spiders, and other invertebrates. Its poison jaws can paralyze prey. A centipede bite may be painful to humans but not lethal. Centipedes prefer the shelter of buildings and darkness and are seldom seen during the day.

Tarantulas (*Dugesiella echina*) are late summer and fall wanderers

Millipedes may reach ten inches in length. These harmless creatures appear in late summer and fall when the summer rainy season begins. Photo by Wauer.

that you are likely to encounter along desert roadways. These giant, hairy spiders are also harmless to humans, but their large size and general appearance make them one of the most feared of the spiders by the uninformed. Although the tarantula will bite in self-defense if treated roughly, its bite is not poisonous. Tarantulas require four or five years to reach full size, and individuals have been known to live for fifteen years. They make good pets and learn to recognize their keeper.

One of the tarantula's more interesting enemies is a large orange and velvet-blue wasp (*Pepsis formosa*) commonly known as the **Tarantula Hawk**. The sting of the "hawk" will not kill the tarantula but will paralyze it. The wasp will then drag the tarantula to a hole or crevice in rocks, sometimes many yards away, where it deposits its eggs in the body of the living spider. The eggs hatch and the wasp larva eat their surroundings. Young wasps finally emerge from the by-then-dead tarantula.

Similar uses of other animals and plants are not unusual in the insect world. In fact, many insects deposit their eggs within or on a particular kind of plant or animal as part of their regular life cycle. If they are unable to locate a host at the proper time, they will die without laying eggs.

Great numbers of wasps utilize plants in this way. "Galls" can be found on most trees and shrubs. Oaks, cottonwoods, persimmon, and even creosote bush have their own species of wasps. Many kinds of galls were eaten by Indians. When ripe with larva, the galls served as nutritional parts of their summer diet.

The large insect order Hymenoptera includes wasps, bees, ants, and their relatives. One of the most curious members of this group is the **Velvet Ant**, which is not an ant at all, but a wasp. These furry little creatures belong to the Mutillidae Family and number 3,000 kinds. Big Bend National Park has several, varying from a large red one (*Dasymutilla klugii*) to a little white one (*D. gloriosa*). These shaggy characters scurry from place to place in search of bee and ant nests where they feed upon the larva. Mutillid males are winged and can be picked up without fear, for they cannot sting. The females, however, pack a real wallop, which you would not readily forget.

Arnold Van Pelt spent the summers of 1969, 1970, and 1971 collecting ants in the Chisos Mountains. He has discovered over 100 species of 30 genera of ants from about 1,500 colonies examined above 4,500 feet elevation. Van Pelt found that different habitats contained distinct assemblages of ants. The habitat with the largest variety of ants was the high woodland canyons where the genera *Monomorium*, *Aphaenogaster*, and *Odotomachus* were most prevalent. Ruderal areas (disturbed areas such as trails) contained an assemblage of *Pogonomyrles* and *Dorymyrmex* genera; grasslands contained *Pogonomyrles* and *Pheidole*; *Liometopum* was restricted to pinyon-juniper-oak slopes; and *Novomessor* was found in arroyos.

In spite of Big Bend's great numbers of interesting and unique invertebrates, little research has been done with these creatures within the park. Only a few of the twenty-six orders of insects have been studied to any degree. Of the many entomologists that have worked in the Texas Big Bend Country, Ernest R. Tinkham was the most productive. His papers on dragonflies (1934), cicads (1941), katydids (1944), and Orthoptera (1948) are major contributions to what has been accomplished in these areas.

Tinkham's 1934 list of nineteen species of dragonflies for the park was increased by Lenora K. Gloyd (1958) who listed thirty-one species.

Theodore J. Cohn (1965) added to the katydid data with his revision of the arid-land katydids of the genus *Neobarraita*. Big Bend National Park has about a dozen species of katydids. One of these—*Paracyrtophyllus excelsus*—is known only from the Chisos Mountains. This is a large green katydid locally known as the **Big Bend Quonker**. Its name was derived from its loud penetrating call, "quonk quonk quonk." Its distinct nighttime call, in the mountain woodlands during late summer and fall, cannot be missed.

The katydid is closely related to the grasshopper. Tinkham summarized all of the grasshoppers known for the Big Bend region in his 1948 article, "Faunistic and Ecological Studies on the Orthoptera of the Big Bend Region of Trans-Pecos Texas, with especial reference to the Orthopteras zones and faunae of midwestern North America." This paper is an essential reference for anyone with a biological interest in this area of the Southwest.

One of the park's most obvious grasshoppers is the **Texas Lubber** (*Taenipoda eques*). This unmistakable creature is a large, heavy-set grasshopper usually found walking on the roads in fall. The body is shiny black, the neck has narrow yellow markings, and the wings are deep rose-red with black edges. The **Texas Toadhopper** (*Phrynotettix robustus*) is another unusual grasshopper, which looks like a little gray toad. Nymphs and adults are stone gray in color and perfectly match their preferred habitat, the limestone slopes of the Dead Horse Mountains. These blunt little creatures are difficult to spot in that environment.

Henry F. Howden (1960) found a new **Long-horned Wood-boring Beetle** (*Cytrinus beckeri*) in dead twigs of Mountain Maples in Pine Canyon and a new **Scarab Beetle** (*Phyllophaga arenicola*) among the mesquites near Boquillas Canyon. Milton W. Sanderson (1948) described two new scarabs from the Chisos Mountains. A new species of soft-bodied beetle (*Oxycopis howdeni*) was described by Ross H. Arnett, Jr. (1965), and Charles A. Triplehorn (1971) described a new Tenebrionidae beetle (*Eleodes knullorum*) from the Chisos Mountains. The Eleodes beetles are a large group that assume a ridiculous position when agitated. Their abdomen is elevated about 45 degrees from the ground, and they seem to be standing on their heads. If disturbed, they emit a dark fluid with a very disagreeable odor, which gave them the common name of "stinkbugs."

Texas Lubber Grasshoppers are common along park roads during late summer and in the fall. Photo by Wauer.

Probably the only group of insects that is reasonably well known in Big Bend National Park is Lepidoptera, the butterflies and moths. Their familiarity is due largely to the work of two researchers who have aggressively studied these groups during the last several years. André Blanchard has collected a total of 387 species of moths from 17 families. In spite of his impressive list of moths for the park, Blanchard said that "there is still much work to be done on Lepidoptera in West Texas and particularly in the Big Bend area."

Roy Kendall prepared a list of 100 species of butterflies and skippers known in the park. Three of these are endemic: the **Chisos Mountains Giant Skipper** (*Agathumus chisosensis* Freeman), **Hafernik's Skipper** (*Piruna haferniki* Freeman), and **Chisos Mountains Metalmark** (*Apodemia chisosensis* Freeman). Kendall has worked out the life history of about 20 percent of Big Bend's skippers and butterflies, and he estimates that eventually 25 additional species will be discovered in the park.

Scorpions are interesting to almost everyone. All are nocturnal in habit and so are rarely seen by the casual visitor to the park. Scorpions live under the bark of dead trees, in crevices in stone and wood, under stones and other debris, and occasionally in human dwellings. All scorpions are venomous. Venom is injected by means of a stinger located at the very tip of the tail. None of the park's scorpions are dangerous to humans; there are no "deadly" scorpions, although any venom can be dangerous if the victim is allergic to it.

At least eleven kinds of scorpions have been found in the park, but it is likely that others will eventually be found, since this is another relatively unexplored group of invertebrates in Big Bend National Park. Two species that are not known to occur elsewhere have been found in the park. W. J. Gertsch (1939) described *Centruroides chisosarius* as a new species; it appears very much like the more poisonous scorpion, *C. sculpturatus*, but has a dark fifth segment of the tail. Otherwise, it is overall dull yellow-cream with a brown back and less than one and a half inches long. The second endemic scorpion is *Diplocentrus bigbendsis*, described by Herbert L. Stahnke (1967). This large scorpion may be three inches in length and is shiny black with dark reddish legs. It is a desert dweller that burrows in the ground, whereas *Centruroides chisosarius* prefers the mountains.

In 1972, Stahnke described two additional scorpions that were found in Big Bend National Park. *Uroctonus apacheanus* occurs from Arizona to the Big Bend Country, and *Vejovis waueri* is known only from southern Texas and adjacent Mexico. This species, originally discovered by W. J. Gertsch in the Chisos Basin, was named for the author.

The common Big Bend scorpion is *Centruroides vittatus*, a rather small, light-colored creature that has been found throughout the park.

Whip scorpions, unlike true scorpions, have no stingers. These large black creatures are also called **Vinegaroons** because of their defensive habit of releasing an odor that is very similar to vinegar. Big Bend's Vinegaroon (*Mastigoproctus giganteus*) is most often found on roadways after dark in summer. It may be six inches in length, although two of those inches may be a thin, whiplike tail. Its pinchers are heavier than those of a scorpion. Although the Vinegaroon is a deadly looking animal, it is not poisonous, and it preys upon insects and other invertebrates that it chases down and captures with its powerful pincers.

Scorpions, whip scorpions, spiders, and mites are all Arachnids, characterized by, among other things, possessing four pairs of legs. The

Sunspider (*Eremobates* sp.) is also an Arachnid. This is another nocturnal creature that looks fearsome but is harmless to humans. Although Sunspiders can bite, they do not possess venom glands. Sunspiders are soft-bodied, light tan animals that may be two to three inches in length.

Very little is known about the park's mites, and most are seldom detected. The **Velvet Mite** (*Dinothrombium* sp.), however, is one of the few that can be seen even during daylight hours, particularly after rain. These bright red little creatures may be locally common. I have seen more than a hundred of them within a few yards along the Rio Grande Village Nature Trail.

Chiggers are larval mites. Richard B. Loomis found forty-one species of chiggers on forty-seven kinds of vertebrate hosts in 1969 and 1970. This field has just begun to develop and has important implications for man's well-being.

Snails are animals that most people associate with ponds and other water areas. However, Big Bend National Park has a fascinating Mollusk fauna. More than two dozen land snails have been recorded within the park. E. P. Cheatum has studied the park's snails for a number of years, and Lloyd Pratt, Jr. has made a thorough study of these animals within the Chisos Mountains. Pratt (1971) described a new species that he found closely associated with Century Plants and restricted to the uplifted block of Boquillas limestone near Laguna Meadow. This creature, the **Agave Snail** (*Humboltiana agovophila*), is round, spherical-shaped, and marked by three brown bands. The common *Humboltiana* of the Chisos Mountains is also an endemic—*H. chisosensis*. It lacks the three brown bands. There are two other endemic *Humboltianas* in the park: *H. edithae* is known only from Emory Peak; and one collected by the author on Sue Peaks, the summit of the Dead Horse Mountains, has not yet been described.

To find such an array of endemics as there is in Big Bend National Park is certainly an indicator of specialized environments. Cheatum found and described *Streptaxis cheatumi* taken from Casa Grande. Two *Holospiras*—very small, long conical shells—have been described from the park as well. *H. riograndensis* is known only from the east side of the Mesa de Anguila, and *H. yucatensis* occurs only on a limestone ridge that extends from near Rio Grande Village across the river into Coahuila, Mexico. Two *Polygyras* are endemic to the park; *P. c. chisosensis* is widely distributed in the Chisos Mountains, and *P. chisosensis discobolus* is known only from upper Blue Creek Canyon.

Bibliography

THE following references are not intended to be a complete list of publications for Big Bend National Park. They represent the major titles, both in print and unpublished, on the topics covered in this book.

Archeology

Bousman, C. Britt, and Margaret Rohrt. 1974. Archeological assessment of Big Bend National Park. Typed report to National Park Service. Arch. Research Program, Southern Methodist University.

Campbell, Tom N. 1967. Archeological survey of the Big Bend National Park, Texas: Part I. Typed report to National Park Service.

————. 1970. Archeological survey of the Big Bend National Park, 1966–1967. Typed report to National Park Service.

Cook, Ruel L. 1937. Archeological survey, Big Bend SP-33-Texas, June 9 to September 3, 1937. Typed report to National Park Service.

Davenport, J. Walker, and Carl Chelf. 1941. Painted pebbles from the lower Pecos and Big Bend regions of Texas. *Witte Mus. Bull.* 5, San Antonio.

Greer, John W. 1965. A typology of midden circles and mescal pits. *Southw. Lore*, 31:41–55.

Griffen, William B. 1969. *Culture changes and shifting populations in central northern Mexico.* Anthro. Papers 13. Tucson: University of Arizona Press.

Harrington, M. R. 1928. A new archeological field in Texas. *Indian Notes*, 5:307–316.

Kelley, J. Charles. 1955. Diffusion in aboriginal Texas. *Amer. Anthro.*, 57:981–995.

Kelley, J. Charles; T. N. Campbell; and D. J. Lehmer. 1940. The association of archeological materials with geological deposits in the Big Bend region of Texas. *Sul Ross Coll. Bull.* 21, no. 3.

Kirkland, Forrest F. 1937. A study of Indian pictures in Texas. *Bull. Texas Arch. Paleo. Soc.* 9:89–119.

Kirkland, Forrest F., and W. W. Newcomb, Jr. 1967. *The rock art of Texas Indians*. Austin: University of Texas Press.

Martin, George C. 1932. The Big Bend basket maker No. 1. *Witte Mus. Bull.* 1, San Antonio.

Newcomb, W. W., Jr. 1961. *The Indians of Texas: From prehistoric to modern times*. Austin: University of Texas Press.

Pearce, J. E. 1938. Geographic influence and civilization with especial reference to Indian Texas. *Texas Geog. Mag.* 2:1–14.

Reed, Erik K. 1936. Special report of archeological work in the Big Bend. Typed report, with photographs, to National Park Service.

Setzler, Frank M. 1935. A prehistoric cave culture in southwestern Texas. *Amer. Anthro.* 37:104–110.

Shafer, Harry J. 1971. *An archeological reconnaissance of the Sanderson Canyon watershed, Texas*. Texas Arch. Salvage Proj. Survey Report no. 7. Austin: University of Texas.

Smith, Victor J. 1932*a*. The relation of the southwestern basket maker to the dry shelter culture of the Big Bend. *Bull. Texas Arch. Paleo. Soc.* 4.

———. 1932*b*. Some notes on dry rock shelters in west Texas. *Amer. Anthro.* 29:2–288.

Suhm, Dee Ann, and Alex D. Kreiger. 1954. An introductory handbook of Texas archeology. *Bull. Texas Arch. Soc.* 25.

Suhm, Dee Ann, and Edward B. Jelks. 1962. *Handbook of Texas archeology: type descriptions*. Austin: Texas Arch. Soc. & Texas Mem. Mus.

Swanton, John R. 1952. *The Indian tribes of North America*. Washington, D.C.: Smithsonian Institution Press.

Wallace, Ernest, and E. Adamson Horbel. 1952. *The Comanches: Lords of the south plains*. Norman: University of Oklahoma Press.

History

Bolton, Herbert E. 1921. *The Spanish borderland*. New Haven: Yale University Press.

Brown, William E., and Roland H. Wauer. 1968. Historic resources management plan for Big Bend National Park. Mimeographed. National Park Service.

Brune, Gunnar. 1975. *Major and historical springs of Texas*. Austin: Texas Water Development Board.

Burgess, Glenn, and Max Bentley. 1947. Father of Big Bend project—E. E. Townsend. *West Texas Today Magazine*, September.

Carroll, J. A. 1968. The Big Bend Country—a regional history. Typed report to National Park Service.

Casey, Clifford B. 1947. The Trans-Pecos in Texas history. Mimeographed.

_____. 1948. Historical—the Big Bend National Park. *Sul Ross State Teachers Coll. Bull.* 28, 2:26–42.

_____. 1967. Castolon. Typed report to National Park Service.

_____. 1968a. Quicksilver mining in the Big Bend of Texas. Typed report to National Park Service.

_____. 1968b. Ranching in the Big Bend. Typed report to National Park Service.

_____. 1969a. Glenn Springs, Texas. Typed report to National Park Service.

_____. 1969b. Soldiers, ranchers and miners in the Big Bend. Mimeographed.

_____. 1970a. The Boquillas–Hot Springs area. Typed report to National Park Service.

_____. 1970b. The candelilla wax industry in the Big Bend Country. Typed report to National Park Service.

_____. 1971. Lajitas, Texas. Typed report to National Park Service.

_____. 1974. *Mirages, mysteries and reality: Brewster County, Texas, the Big Bend of the Rio Grande*. Sitgreaves, Texas: Pioneer Book Publishers.

Cash, Joseph H., and Gerald W. Wolff. 1974. *The Comanche people*. Phoenix: Indian Tribal Service.

Corning, Paul. 1967. *Baronial forts of the Big Bend*. San Antonio: Trinity University Press.

Cramer, Stuart W. 1916. Punitive expedition from Boquillas. *U.S. Cavalry J.* 28 (Oct.):200–227.

Davis, Donald G. 1969. Remains of early telephone lines in Big Bend National Park. Typed report to National Park Service.

Dobyns, Henry F. 1973. *The Mescalero Apache people*. Phoenix: Indian Tribal Service.

Easterla, Patricia James. 1968. Big Bend of yesterday. *Nat. Parks Mag.* 42:4–8.

Echols, William H. 1860. Report of Oct. 10, including diary and map. U.S. Congress, Senate Doc., 36th Cong., 2d sess., vol. 60.

Edwards, Cas. 1951. Story of Glenn Springs raid as told by eye witness of border murders. *Alpine Avalanche,* vol. 60, Sept. 14.

Emory, William Hemsley. 1951. *Lieutenant Emory reports.* Albuquerque: University of New Mexico Press.

Fulcher, Walter. 1959. *The way I heard it: Tales of the Big Bend.* Austin: University of Texas Press.

Garrison, L. A. 1953. A history of the proposed Big Bend International Park. Mimeographed report to National Park Service.

Gillette, James B. 1933. The old G4 ranch. *Voice of the Mexican Border* 2:82–83.

Goetzmann, William H. 1959. *Army exploration in the American west, 1803–1863.* New Haven: Yale University Press.

Hartz, Edward L. 1859. Diary report of camel travel through Big Bend area. Report of Sec. of War, Senate Executive Documents no. 2, 36th Cong., 1st Sess.

Hawley, C. A. 1964. Life along the border. *Sul Ross State Teachers Coll. Bull.* 44:7–87.

Hill, Robert T. 1901. Running the canyons of the Rio Grande. *Century Mag.* 61:371–387.

Hine, Robert V. 1968. *Bartlett's west —Drawing the Mexican boundary.* New Haven: Yale University Press.

Hinkle, Stacy C. 1967. *Wings and saddles: the air and cavalry punitive expedition of 1919.* University of Texas at El Paso Southwestern Studies, Monograph 19. El Paso: Texas Western Press.

Hitchcock, Nelle Totsy. 1965. Castolon research. Typed report to National Park Service.

———. 1966. Some Big Bend personalities, 1895–1925. Master's thesis, Sul Ross State College.

Jameson, John R., Sr. 1974. Big Bend National Park of Texas: A brief history of the formative years, 1930–1952. Ph.D. dissertation, University of Toledo.

Langford, J. O. 1952. *Big Bend —a homesteader's story.* Austin: University of Texas Press.

Levy, Benjamin. 1968. Hot Springs, Big Bend National Park. Historic Structures Report, National Park Service.

McGee, Bernice, and Jack McGee. 1972. Mystery tablet of the Big Bend. *True West*, July-August, pp. 10–15, 42–50.

Madison, Virginia. 1968. *The Big Bend Country.* New York: October House.

Madison, Virginia, and Hallie Stillwell. 1958. *How come it's called that?* New York: October House.

Maxwell, Ross A. 1968. *The Big Bend of the Rio Grande.* Austin: Bur. Econ. Geol., Guidebook No. 7.

Maxwell, Ross A.; J. T. Lonsdale; R. T. Hazzard; and J. A. Wilson. 1967. *Geology of Big Bend National Park, Brewster County, Texas.* Publication no. 6711. Austin: Bur. Econ. Geol., Univ. Tex.

Mellerd, Evelyn. 1964. High ground in Texas. *Sul Ross State Teachers Coll. Bull.* 44:89–127.

Mellerd, Rudolph. 1964. *Hills and horizons.* San Antonio: Naylor.

Miles, Elton. 1976. *Tales of the Big Bend.* College Station: Texas A&M University Press.

Morelock, H. W. 1938. Proposed Big Bend National Park. *Texas Geog. Mag.* 2:13–18.

Newsmith, H. M. 1911. Early days on the border. *Texas Mag.* 3:21–25.

Newsome, C. M. "Buck." 1975. *Shod with iron.* Marfa: Private publication.

Prewitt, Ray A. 1947. A summary of the predominant economic activities peculiar to the Big Bend area prior to its establishment as a national park and some of the economic effects of the park on the surrounding region. Typed report to National Park Service.

Raborg, William A. 1954. The Villa raid on Glenn Springs. Mimeographed.

Raht, Carlysle G. 1919. *The romance of Davis Mountains and Big Bend Country.* Odessa: Rahtbooks.

Ribby, Fred J. 1919. The Indians of the Southwest in the diplomacy of the United States and Mexico, 1848–1853. *Hispanic Amer. Hist. Rev.* 2: 363–396.

Saxton, Lewis H., and Clifford B. Casey. 1958. *The life of Everett Ewing Townsend.* West Texas Hist. & Acad. Soc., no. 17. Alpine: Sul Ross State College.

Sheire, James, and Robert V. Simmonds. 1973. Historic structure report, Castolon Army Compound, Big Bend National Park, Texas. Denver: National Park Service.

Smithers, W. D. 1958. Hay from the mountain tops. *Cattleman* 45:39–42.

———. 1961a. The border trading posts. *Sul Ross State Coll. Bull.* 41, 3: 41–61.

———. 1961b. Nature's pharmacy and the curanderos. *Sul Ross State Coll. Bull.* 41, 3:15–40.

———. 1961c. Pancho Villa's last hangout. *Sul Ross State Coll. Bull.* 41, 3:62–112.

———. 1963. Bandit raids in the Big Bend Country. *Sul Ross State Coll. Bull.* 44, 3:75–105.

———. 1976. *Chronicles of the Big Bend.* Austin: University of Texas Press.

Sonnichsen, Charles L. 1950. *Cowboys and cattle kings.* Norman: University of Oklahoma Press.

Swarthout, Glendon. 1972. *The tin lizzie troop.* New York: Pocket Books.

Townsend, E. E. 1935. Rangers and Indians in the Big Bend region. *Sul Ross State Teachers Coll. Bull.* 56:43–48.

Tyler, Ronnie C. 1968. Exploring the Rio Grande—Lt. Duff C. Green's report of 1852. *Quart. J. Hist. Univ. Arizona.* 10 (Spring):43–60.

———. 1975a. *The Big Bend, a history of the last Texas frontier.* Washington, D.C.: National Park Service.

———. 1975b. The little punitive expedition in the Big Bend. *Southw. Hist. Quart.* 78:273–291.

Utley, Robert M. 1962. Longhorns of the Big Bend. Typed report to National Park Service.

Weedin, Teresa J. 1975. Historic ruins along the middle Tornillo Creek, Big Bend National Park, Texas: a look at times gone by, 1880–1942. Paper presented to the Texas Archeological Society meeting, October 31–November 2, 1975, San Antonio.

Wegemann, Carroll H. 1936. Diary of a trip from Alpine, Texas to the Big Bend and old Mexico with the International Park Commission. Typed report, with photographs, to National Park Service.

Williams, O. H. 1966. *Pioneer surveyor—frontier lawyer.* El Paso: West Texas Press.

Wood, C. D. 1963. The Glenn Springs raid. *Sul Ross State Coll. Bull.* 44, 3:65–71.

Wright, Mrs. Joel E. 1963. Early settling of the Big Bend. *Sul Ross State Coll. Bull.* 43, 3:55–62.

Ecology

Applegate, Howard G. 1970. Residues in fish, wildlife, and estuaries. Insecticides in the Big Bend National Park. *Pesticides Monitoring J.* 4, 1:2–7.

Bailey, Vernon. 1905. Biological survey of Texas. *N. Amer. Fauna*, no. 25.

Baker, Rollin H. 1958. The future of wildlife in northern Mexico—a problem of conservation education. *Trans. 23rd N. Amer. Wildl. Conf.*, pp. 567–575.

Blair, Frank W. 1950. The biotic provinces of Texas. *Texas J. Sci.* 2:93–117.

Bray, William L. 1901. The ecological relations of the vegetation of western Texas. *Bot. Gaz.* 32:99–291.

Bryant, Vaughn B., Jr., 1977. Late quaternary pollen records from the east-central periphery of the Chihuahuan Desert. In *Trans. Sympos. Biol. Resources Chihuahuan Desert Region, U.S. and Mexico*, edited by Roland H. Wauer and David H. Riskind. USDI, National Park Service Trans. Proc. Ser. No. 3.

Carter, W. T. 1928. Soil survey (reconnaissance) of the Trans-Pecos area, Texas. *Bull. Univ. Tex. Sci. Ser.* 35:1–66.

Carter, W. T., and V. L. Cory. 1931. Soils of the Trans-Pecos, Texas, and some of their vegetative relations. *Trans. Texas Acad. Sci.* 15:19–37.

Chew, R. M., and A. E. Chew. 1965. The primary productivity of a desert shrub (*Larrea tridentata*) community. *Ecol. Monog.* 35:355–375.

Cottle, H. J. 1931. Studies in the vegetation of southwestern Texas. *Ecology* 12:105–155.

Coulter, John M. 1894. *Botany of western Texas.* Contr. U.S. Nat. Herb. 19.

Degenhardt, William G. 1977. A changing environment: documentation of lizards and plants over a decade. In *Trans. Sympos. Biol. Resources Chihuahuan Desert Region, U.S. and Mexico*, edited by Roland H. Wauer and David H. Riskind. USDI, National Park Service Trans. Proc. Ser. No. 3.

Denyes, H. A. 1956. Natural terrestrial communities of Brewster County, Texas, with special reference to the distribution of the mammals. *Amer. Midl. Nat.* 55:289–320.

Dice, J. R. 1943. *The biotic provinces of North America.* Ann Arbor: University of Michigan Press.

Dick-Peddie, William A., and Michael S. Alberico. 1977. Fire ecology study of the Chisos Mountains, Big Bend National Park, Texas. Typed report to National Park Service.

Ditton, Robert B., and A. R. Graefe. 1976. An approach for evaluating recreational impact on river resources in Big Bend National Park. 8th Recreation Mgt. Inst., Water Rec. Resources: planning, development, management. Texas A&M University.

Ditton, Robert B.; A. R. Graefe; and T. Mertens. 1977. River road camping in Big Bend National Park: a survey and analysis. Typed report to National Park Service.

Ditton, Robert B.; D. J. Schmidly; W. J. Boeer; and A. R. Graefe. 1977. A survey and analysis of recreational and livestock impact on the riparian zone of the Rio Grande in Big Bend National Park. Proc. Symp. River Rec. Mgt. & Res., Jan. 1977, Texas A&M University.

Dixon, Keith L., et al. 1957. Ecological survey of the Big Bend area. Texas A&M University, mimeographed.

Dumas, Gerald A. 1974. Determination of submicrogram quantities of mercury in the Rough Run–Terlingua Creek area of the Big Bend Region of Texas. Master's thesis, Sul Ross State University.

Gallagher, Daniel S. 1974. Mercury concentrations in lizards collected from the Terlingua mining district of Trans-Pecos Texas. Master's thesis, Sul Ross State University.

Gardner, J. L. 1950. Effects of thirty years of protection from grazing in desert grassland. *Ecology* 31:44–50.

Gehlbach, Frederick R. 1962. Chihuahuan and Sonoran desert vegetation: some basic considerations. Mimeographed.

––––––. 1965. Plant ecology of the Boot Canyon and McKittrick Canyon trails, Trans-Pecos, Texas. Typed report to National Park Service.

––––––. 1966a. Biomes of the Big Bend, Texas: a preliminary descriptive outline. Paper presented to Ecology Study Group, Baylor University.

––––––. 1966b. Plant formation in the natural history interpretation of the southwestern desert regions. *Nat. Parks Mag.* 40:16–18.

Gould, F. W. 1969. *Texas plants—a checklist and ecological summary.* 2d ed. College Station, Tex.: Texas Agri. Exp. Stat., Texas A&M University.

Graefe, A. R. 1977. Elements of motivation and satisfaction in the float trip experience in Big Bend National Park. Master's thesis, Texas A&M University.

Harris, Arthur H. 1977. Wisconsin age environments in the northern Chihuahuan Desert: evidence from the higher vertebrates. In *Trans. Sympos. Biol. Resources Chihuahuan Desert Region, U.S. and Mexico,* edited by

Roland H. Wauer and David H. Riskind. USDI, National Park Service Trans. Proc. Ser. No. 3.

Hendrickson, James, and R. M. Straw. 1976. A gazetteer of the Chihuahuan Desert region, a supplement to the Chihuahuan Desert flora. Los Angeles: California State University.

Houston, James G. 1975. Mercury study in Big Bend. Typed report to National Park Service.

Houston, James G., and G. A. Dumas. 1974. Mercury study in the Rough Run–Terlingua Creek and Rio Grande areas of Big Bend National Park, Texas. Typed report to National Park Service.

Humphrey, Robert R. 1958. *The desert grassland.* Tucson: University of Arizona Press.

Hunt, W. Grainger. 1974. The significance of wilderness ecosystems in western Texas and adjacent regions in the ecology of the Peregrine. Typed report to National Park Service.

Jaeger, Edmund C. 1957. *The North American deserts.* Stanford: Stanford University Press.

Johnson, Maynard. 1937. Preliminary report of a wildlife survey of the Big Bend National Park, Texas. Typed report to National Park Service.

Judd, Frank W.; A. Sartain; and W. Phillips. 1966. A preliminary reconnaissance of Dagger Flat, Big Bend National Park, Brewster County, Texas. Typed reports to National Park Service.

Kittams, Walter H. 1972. Effect of fire on vegetation of the Chihuahuan Desert region. *Proc. Tall Timbers Fire Ecol. Conf.* 12:427–444.

Leopold, A. Starker. 1950. Vegetation zones of Mexico. *Ecology* 31:507–518.

Lind, Owen T., and C. A. Bane. 1975. A limnological survey of aquatic resources of the Rio Grande Valley in Big Bend National Park between Hot Springs and Boquillas Canyon. Typed report to National Park Service.

McDougall, W. B. 1953a. Ecology—Big Bend National Park. Typed report to National Park Service.

———. 1953b. Preliminary report on a plant ecological survey of the Big Bend area of Texas. Typed report to National Park Service.

Marsh, Ernest G., Jr. 1936. Biological survey of the Santa Rosa and del Carmen mountains of northern Coahuila, Mexico. Typed report to National Park Service.

———. 1938. An ecological report of the flora of the Big Bend area. Typed report to National Park Service.

Meyer, Edward R. 1977. A reconnaissance survey of pollen rain in Big Bend National Park, Texas: modern control for a paleo-environmental study. In *Trans. Sympos. Biol. Resources Chihuahuan Desert Region, U.S. and Mexico*, edited by Roland H. Wauer and David H. Riskind. USDI, National Park Service Trans. Proc. Ser. No. 3.

Milstead, William W. 1960. Relict species of the Chihuahuan Desert. *Southw. Nat.* 5:75–88.

Muller, C. H. 1940. Plant succession in the *Larrea-Flourensia* climax. *Ecology* 21:206–212.

Palmer, Ernest J. 1928. A botanical trip through the Chisos Mountains of Texas. *J. Arnold Arbor.* 9:153–173.

Powell, A. Michael, and B. L. Turner. 1977. Aspects of the plant biology of the gypsum outcrops of the Chihuahuan Desert. In *Trans. Sympos. Biol. Resources Chihuahuan Desert Region, U.S. and Mexico*, edited by Roland H. Wauer and David H. Riskind. USDI, National Park Service Trans. Proc. Ser. No. 3.

Rowell, Chester M., Jr. 1967. The Chihuahuan Desert in Texas. Mimeographed.

Schmidly, David J., and Robert B. Ditton. 1976. A survey and analysis of recreational and livestock impacts on the riparian zone of the Rio Grande in Big Bend National Park. Typed report to National Park Service.

Schmidly, David J.; R. B. Ditton; W. J. Boeer; and A. R. Graefe. 1979. Inter-relationships among visitor usage, human impact, and the biotic resources of the riparian ecosystem in Big Bend National Park. *Proc. First Conf. Sci. Res. in National Parks, November, 1976*, edited by Robert M. Linn. USDI, National Park Service Trans. Proc. Ser. No. 5.

Schulman, Edmund. 1952. Dendrochronology in Big Bend National Park, Texas. *Tree-ring Bull.* 18:18–27.

————. 1954. Rio Grande chronologies. *Tree-ring Bull.* 20.

Shelford, Victor E. 1963. *The ecology of North America*. Urbana: University of Illinois Press.

Shreve, Forrest. 1939. Observations on the vegetation of Chihuahua. *Madrono* 5:1–13.

————. 1942a. The desert vegetation of North America. *Bot. Rev.* 8:195–246.

————. 1942b. Grassland and related vegetation in northern Mexico. *Madrono* 6:190–198.

Shreve, Forrest, and A. L. Hinckley. 1937. Thirty years of change in desert vegetation. *Ecology* 18:463–478.

Smith, Tarleton. 1936. Wildlife report on the proposed Big Bend National Park. Typed report to National Park Service.

Sperry, O. E. 1938. Report of the biological consultant for the proposed Big Bend National Park area of Texas. Typed report to National Park Service.

Stevenson, J. O. 1935. General wildlife considerations of the Big Bend area of Texas. Typed report to National Park Service.

Taylor, Walter P.; W. B. McDougall; and W. B. Davis. 1944. Preliminary report on an ecological survey of Big Bend National Park. Typed report to Fish and Wildlife Service.

Taylor, Walter P.; W. B. McDougall; C. C. Presnell; and K. P. Schmidt. 1946. The Sierra del Carmen in northern Coahuila, a preliminary ecological survey. *Texas Geog. Mag.* 10, 1:11–22.

Thompson, Ben H. 1934. Report upon the wildlife of the Big Bend area of the Rio Grande, Texas. Typed report to National Park Service.

Visher, Stephen S. 1949. American dry seasons—their intensity and frequency. *Ecology* 30:365–370.

Warnock, Barton H. 1967. Photographic vegetation study, Big Bend National Park. Mimeographed report to National Park Service.

———. 1969. Vegetation survey—Big Bend National Park. Mimeographed report to National Park Service.

Wauer, Roland H. 1970. The history of land use and some ecological implications, Big Bend National Park, Texas. Typed report to National Park Service.

———. 1971. Preliminary ecological survey of the Lower Canyons of the Rio Grande. Typed report to National Park Service.

———. 1974. Changes in the breeding avifauna within the Chisos Mountains system. Typed report to National Park Service.

———. 1975a. A case history of land use and some ecological implications— the Chisos Mountains, Big Bend National Park, Texas. *Proc. 2nd Nat. Res. Conf.*, 1975. Southwest Regional Office, National Park Service.

———. 1975b. Management of non-game birds in current policies and decision making within the National Park Service. *Proc. Sympos. Mgt. Forest & Range Habitat for Nongame Birds.* USDA, Forest Service, Gen. Tech. Report WO-1.

Wells, Philip V. 1966. Late Pleistocene vegetation and degree of pluvial climatic change in the Chihuahuan Desert. *Science* 153:970–975.

_____. 1970. Postglacial vegetational history of the Great Plains. *Science* 167:1574–1582.

_____. 1977. Post-glacial origin of the present Chihuahuan Desert less than 11,500 years ago. In *Trans. Sympos. Biol. Resources Chihuahuan Desert Region, U.S. and Mexico,* edited by Roland H. Wauer and David H. Riskind. USDI, National Park Service Trans. Proc. Ser. No. 3.

West, Robert C., ed. 1964. *Natural environment and early cultures. Handbook of Middle American Indians.* Vol. 1. Austin: University of Texas Press.

Whitson, Paul D. 1965. Phytocoecology of Boot Canyon woodland, Chisos Mountains, Big Bend National Park. Master's thesis, Baylor University.

_____. 1970. Dynamics of the shrub desert formation, succulent desert formation transition in Big Bend National Park, Texas. Ph.D. dissertation, University of Oklahoma.

_____. 1974. *The impact of human use upon the Chisos Basin and adjacent lands.* USDI, National Park Service Monog. Ser. No. 4.

Yang, T. W. 1961. The recent expansion of creosotebush (*Larrea divaricata*) in the North American desert. *West. Res., Nat. Hist. Mus. Spec. Publ.* 1.

_____. 1970. Major chromosome races of *Larrea divaricata* in North America. *J. Ariz. Acad. Sci.* 6:41–45.

Botany

Adams, R. P. 1975*a*. Gene flow versus selection pressure and ancestral differentiation in the composition of species; analysis of populational variation of *Juniperus ashei* Buch. using terpenoid data. *J. Mol. Evol.* 5:177–185.

_____. 1975*b*. Numerical-chemosystematic studies of infraspecific variation in *Juniperus pinchotii. Biochem. System. Ecol.* 3:71–74.

Adams, R. P., and A. Hagerman. 1976. A comparison of the volatile oils of mature versus young leaves of *Juniperus scopulorum*: chemosystematic significance. *Biochem. System. Ecol.* 4:75–79.

Anderson, Edward F. 1963. A revision of *Ariocarpus* (Cactaceae). III. Formal taxonomy of the subgenus Rosecactus. *Amer. J. Bot.* 50:724–732.

_____. 1964. A revision of *Ariocarpus* (Cactaceae). IV. Formal taxonomy of the subgenus *Ariocarpus. Amer. J. Bot.* 51:144–151.

Anthony, Margery. 1954. Ecology of the *Opuntiae* in the Big Bend region of Texas. *Ecology* 35:334–347.

_____. 1956. The *Opuntiae* of the Big Bend region of Texas. *Amer. Midl. Nat.* 55:225–256.

Barbour, M. G. 1969a. Age and space distribution of some desert shrub *Larrea divaricata*. *Ecology* 50:679–685.

_____. 1969b. Patterns of genetic similarity between *Larrea divaricata* of North and South America. *Amer. Midl. Nat.* 81:54–67.

Beitung, August J. 1968. The agaves. *Cactus Suc. J. Yearbook.*

Benson, Lyman. 1968a. The cacti of the United States and Canada, new names and nomenclature combinations. *Cactus Suc. J.* 41:124–228.

_____. 1968b. The complexity of species and the varieties of *Echinocereus pectinatus*. *Cactus Suc. J.* 40:119–127.

Benson, Lyman, and R. A. Darrow. 1954. *The trees and shrubs of southwestern deserts*. Albuquerque: University of New Mexico Press.

Boke, Norman H. 1955. Diomorphic areoles of *Epithelantha*. *Amer. J. Bot.* 42:725–733.

_____. 1957a. Comparative histogensis of areoles in *Homalocephala* and *Echinocactus*. *Amer. J. Bot.* 44:368–380.

_____. 1957b. Evidence for the recognition of two species of *Epithelantha* in the Big Bend of Texas. Mimeographed.

Bray, William L. 1905. Vegetation of the Sotol country in Texas. *Bull. Univ. Texas Sci. Ser.* 6:1–24.

Brown, Stanley D. 1965. A new cactus alkaloid. Master's thesis, Texas Christian University.

Burr, Eric. 1966. Aspen survey. Typed report to National Park Service.

Conde, Louis F. 1972. Anatomical comparisons of some *Cylindro-* and *Platyopuntias*. Ph.D. dissertation, Duke University.

Correll, Donovan S. 1956. *Ferns and fern allies of Texas*. Renner: Texas Research Foundation.

_____. 1959. An interesting holanthoid plant in Texas. *Wrightia* 2, 1:43.

_____. 1965. Some additions and corrections to the flora of Texas. *Wrightia* 3:126–140.

Correll, Donovan S., and M. C. Johnston. 1970. *Manual of the vascular plants of Texas*. Renner: Texas Research Foundation.

Craig, Robert T. 1945. *The Mammillaria handbook*. Pasadena, Calif.: Abbey Garden Press.

Cummins, George B. 1964. Uredinales of the Big Bend National Park and adjacent areas of Texas. *Southw. Nat.* 8:181–195.

————. 1965. Additional Uredinales of the Big Bend area of Texas. *Southw. Nat.* 10:35–38.

Davis, Donald G. 1969. Habitat of the night-blooming Cereus (*Cereus greggii*) in the Marathon Basin, Texas. Typed report to National Park Service.

Foster, William J. 1973. A study of the medicinal plants in Trans-Pecos region and the Big Bend National Park area of west Texas. Master's thesis, Sul Ross State University.

Freeman, C. E. 1973*a*. Germination responses of a Texas population of Ocotillo (*Fouquieria splendens* Engelm.) to constant temperature, water stress, pH and salinity. *Amer. Midl. Nat.* 89:252–256.

————. 1973*b*. Some germination responses of Lechuguilla (*Agave lecheguilla* Torr.). *Southw. Nat.* 18:125–134.

Gamer, Eleanor E. 1966. Big Bend and the botanist. *Nat. Parks Mag.* 40:14–17.

Goggans, James E., and C. E. Posey. 1968. Variation in seeds and ovulate cones of some species and varieties of *Cupressus*. Auburn Univ. Exp. Stat. Circul. 160.

Gould, F. W. 1951. *Grasses of southwestern United States*. Tucson: University of Arizona Press.

Green, Anthony W. 1969. The ecology and distribution of *Hechtia scariosa* in the Big Bend National Park. Master's thesis, Sul Ross State University.

Havard, V. 1885. Report on the flora of southern and western Texas. *U.S. Nat. Mus.* 8:449–533.

Horner, Harry T., Jr., and C. K. Beltz. 1970. Cellular differentiations of Heterospory in Selaginella. *Protoplasma* 71:335–341.

Irwin, Howard S. 1961. *Roadside flowers of Texas*. Austin: University of Texas Press.

Johnston, Marshall C. 1962*a*. The North American mesquites *Prosopis* Sect. *Algarobia* (Leguminosa). *Brittonia* 14:72–90.

————. 1962*b*. Revision of Condalia including Microrhamnus (Rhamnacae). *Brittonia* 14:332–368.

————. 1977. Brief resume of botanical, including vegetational, features of the Chihuahuan Desert region with special emphasis on their uniqueness. In *Trans. Sympos. Biol. Resources Chihuahuan Desert Region, U.S. and Mexico*, edited by Roland H. Wauer and David H. Riskind. USDI, National Park Service Trans. Proc. Ser. No. 3.

Johnston, Marshall C., and B. H. Warnock. 1962a. The four species of *Acalypha* (Euphorbiaceae) in far western Texas. *Southw. Nat.* 7:182–190.

_____. 1962b. The ten species of *Croton* (Euphorbiaceae) in far western Texas. *Southw. Nat.* 7:1–22.

McDougall, W. B., and O. E. Sperry. 1951. Plants of Big Bend National Park. Washington, D.C.: Government Printing Office.

Magill, R. E. 1972. Preliminary checklist of Big Bend National Park moss flora. Typed report to National Park Service.

Mahler, W. F. 1971. Key to the vascular plants of the Black Gap Wildlife Management Area, Brewster County, Texas. Dallas: Southern Methodist University Press.

Mahler, W. F., and U. T. Waterfall. 1964. *Baccharis* (Compositae) in Oklahoma, Texas and New Mexico. *Southw. Nat.* 9:189–200.

Marshall, W. Taylor. 1940. *Echinocereus Chisosensis. Cactus Suc. J.* 12:15.

Moore, Winifred O. 1967. The *Echinocereus enneacanthus—dubius—stramineus* complex (Cactacea). *Brittonia* 19:77–79.

Muller, C. H. 1937. Vegetation in Chisos Mountains, Texas. *Trans. Texas Acad. Sci.* 20:3–31.

_____. 1939. A new species of Agave from Trans-Pecos Texas. *Amer. Midl. Nat.* 21:763–765.

_____. 1951. *The oaks of Texas.* Renner: Texas Research Foundation.

Newman, Nicholas G. 1967. The wax makers. *Nat. Parks Mag.* 41:14–15.

Niles, Wesley Everett. 1970. Taxonomic investigations in the genera *Perityle* and *Laphamis* (Compositae). *Memoirs N.Y. Bot. Garden* 21:1–82.

O'Neill, Earl W., III. 1971. An ecological investigation of the giant dagger (*Yucca carnerosana*) in Big Bend National Park, Brewster, Texas. Master's thesis, Sul Ross State University.

Parmalee, J. A. 1967. The autoecious species of Pucciria on *Heliantheae* in North America. *Canadian J. Bot.* 45:2267–2327.

Peattie, Donald Culross. 1953. *A natural history of western trees.* Boston: Houghton-Mifflin Co.

Pennell, Francis W. 1941. Scrophulaciaeae of Trans-Pecos Texas. *Proc. Acad. Nat. Sci. Phil.* 62:289–308.

Posey, Clayton E., and J. E. Goggans. 1967. Observations of species of Cypress indigenous to the United States. Auburn Univ. Agri. Exp. Stat. Circ. 153.

Riskind, David H. 1971. Some preliminary observations on the vegetation of the Lower Canyons of the Rio Grande, Brewster and Terrell Counties, Texas, and Coahuila, Mexico. Typed report to Bureau of Outdoor Recreation.

———. 1973a. Species list of plants observed and/or collected in the Lower Canyons of the Rio Grande: Black Gap Wildlife Refuge–Dryden Crossing, March 31–April 15, 1973. Typed report to Bureau of Outdoor Recreation.

———. 1973b. A vegetation survey of the Lower Canyons of the Rio Grande, March 31–April 6, 1973. Typed report to Bureau of Outdoor Recreation.

Roseberry, R. D., and N. E. Dole, Jr. 1938. Big Bend vegetative type map report. Typed report to National Park Service.

Ruth, Harry R. 1972. A study of the stomata of two Big Bend monocotyledons. Typed report to National Park Service.

Schulz, Ellen D. 1930. Texas cacti. *Proc. Texas Acad. Sci.*, vol. 14.

Smith, Cornelia M., and G. A. Smith. 1970. An electrophoretic comparison of six species of Yucca and of Hesperaloe. *Bot. Gaz.* 131:201–205.

Sperry, Omer E. 1938. A check list of the ferns, gymnosperms, and flowering plants of the proposed Big Bend National Park. *Sul Ross State Teachers Coll. Bull.* 19, 4:9–98.

———. 1941. Additions to the check list of plants of the proposed Big Bend National Park area. *Sul Ross State Coll. Bull.* 22, 1:9–60.

Sperry, Omer E., and B. H. Warnock. 1941. Plants of Brewster County. *Sul Ross State Coll. Bull.* 22:17–60.

Tharp, Benjamin Carroll. 1939. *The vegetation of Texas.* Houston: Anson Jones Press.

Thompson, Henry J., and J. E. Zavortink. 1968. Two new species of *Mentzelia* in Texas. *Wrightia* 4:21–24.

Turner, B. L. 1959. *The legumes of Texas.* Austin: University of Texas Press.

Vines, Robert A. 1960. *Trees, shrubs, and woody vines of the Southwest.* Austin: University of Texas Press.

Warnock, Barton H., and M. C. Johnston. 1960. The genus *Savia* (Euphorbiaceae) in extreme west Texas. *Southw. Nat.* 5:1–6.

Warnock, Barton H., and P. Koch. 1970. *Wildflowers of the Big Bend Country, Texas.* Alpine: Sul Ross State University.

———. 1974. *Wildflowers of the Guadalupe Mountains and the Sand Dune Country, Texas.* Alpine: Sul Ross State University.

_____. 1977. *Wildflowers of the Davis Mountains and the Marathon Basin, Texas.* Alpine: Sul Ross State University.

Wauer, Roland H. 1970. Cactaceae (other than *Opuntia*) of Big Bend National Park. Typed report to National Park Service.

_____. 1971. Oaks of Big Bend National Park. Typed report to National Park Service.

Wells, Philip V. 1965. Vegetation of the Dead Horse Mountains, Brewster County, Texas. *Southw. Nat.* 10:256–260.

Weniger, Del. 1970. *Cacti of the Southwest.* Austin: University of Texas Press.

Wetmore, Clifford M. 1976. Macrolichens of Big Bend National Park, Texas. *The Bryologist* 79:296–313.

Whitehouse, Eula, and F. McAllister. 1954. The mosses of Texas. *The Bryologist* 57:53–146.

Yang, T. W. 1967. Chromosome numbers in populations of creosotebush (*Larrea divaricata*) in the Chihuahuan and Sonoran subdivision of the North American desert. *J. Arizona Acad. Sci.* 4:183–184.

Zanoni, Thomas A., and R. P. Adams. 1975. The genus *Juniperus* (Cupressaceae) in Mexico and Guatemala: numerical and morphological analysis. *Boletín Societe Botanica de México*, no. 35:69–92.

_____. 1976. The genus *Juniperus* in Mexico and Guatemala: numerical and chemosystematic analysis. *Biochem. System. Ecol.* 4:147–158.

Mammals

Atkinson, Don E. 1976. Population dynamics and predator-prey relationships of the Carmen Mountains white-tailed deer. Master's thesis, Texas A&M University.

Baccus, John T. 1971. The influence of a return of native grasslands upon the ecology and distribution of small rodents in Big Bend National Park. Ph.D. dissertation, North Texas State University.

_____. 1973. Additional data on the ecology of small mammals in Big Bend National Park. Typed report to National Park Service.

Baker, Rollin H. 1956. Mammals of Coahuila, Mexico. *Univ. Kansas Publ., Mus. Nat. Hist.* 9:125–335.

Barbour, Roger W., and W. H. Davis. 1969. *Bats of America.* Lexington: University Press of Kentucky.

Bissonnette, J. A. 1974a. The relationship of resource quality and availability to social behavior and organization in collared peccary. Ph.D. dissertation, University of Michigan.

———. 1974*b*. The status of biological research in Big Bend National Park, Texas, with special reference to mammals. Typed report to National Park Service.

Blackman, John N. 1970. A survey of forage and eating preferences of the Carmen white-tailed deer, Big Bend National Park. Master's thesis, Sul Ross State University.

Blair, Frank W. 1949. Shade of pelage color in two populations of kangaroo rats and remarks on the status of *Dipodomys merriami ambiguous* Merriam. *J. Mamm.* 30:388–390.

———. 1954. A melanistic race of the white-throated packrat (*Neotoma albigula*) in Texas. *J. Mamm.* 35:239–242.

Blair, Frank W., and C. E. Miller, Jr. 1949. The mammals of the Sierra Vieja region, southwestern Texas, with remarks on the biological positions of the region. *Texas J. Sci.* 1:67–91.

Boeer, William J., and D. J. Schmidly. 1977. Terrestrial mammals of the riparian corridor, in Big Bend National Park. In *Importance, preservation, and management of riparian habitat: a symposium.* USDA, Forest Service, Gen. Tech. Report RM-43.

Borell, A. E., and M. D. Bryant. 1942. Mammals of the Big Bend area of Texas. *Univ. California Publ. Zool.* 48:1–62.

Bryant, M. D. 1939. A new kangaroo rat of the *Dipodomys ordii* group from the Big Bend region of Texas. *Occas. Publ. Mus. Zool. Louisiana State Univ.* 5:65–66.

Buechner, H. K. 1950. Life history, ecology, and range use of the pronghorn antelope in Trans-Pecos Texas. *Amer. Midl. Nat.* 43:257–354.

Carson, Burch. 1941. Man, the greatest enemy of desert bighorn mountain sheep. *Texas Game, Fish and Oyster Comm. Bull.* 21:5–23.

Constantine, Denny C. 1961. Locality records and notes on western bats. *J. Mamm.* 43:404–405.

Crowder, Rod L. 1969. A revised study of *Castor canadensis Mexicanus*. Typed report to Sul Ross State College.

———. 1970. An ecological study of *Sigmodon ochrognathus*. Master's thesis, Sul Ross State University.

Davis, William B. 1960. *The mammals of Texas.* Austin: Texas Game and Fish Commission.

———. 1974. The mammals of Texas (revised). *Texas Parks and Wildlife Dept. Bull.* 41.

Davis, William B. and W. P. Taylor. 1939. The bighorn sheep of Texas. *J. Mamm.* 20:440–455.

Dixon, Keith L. 1959. Spatial organization in a population of Nelson pocket mouse. *Southw. Nat.* 3:107–113.

Easterla, David A. 1968*a*. First record of the pocketed free-tailed bat for Texas. *J. Mamm.* 49:515–516.

_____. 1968*b*. Species and numbers of bats banded at Big Bend National Park, Rosillos Ranch, and Fern Canyon (Chihuahua, Mexico), Brewster County, Texas. Typed report to National Park Service.

_____. 1970*a*. First record of the pocketed free-tailed bat for Coahuila, Mexico, and additional Texas records. *Texas J. Sci.* 22:92–93.

_____. 1970*b*. First record of the spotted bat in Texas and notes on its natural history. *Amer. Midl. Nat.* 83:306–308.

_____. 1971. Notes on young and adults of the spotted bat, *Euderma maculatum. J. Mamm.* 52:475–476.

_____. 1972*a*. A diurnal colony of big free-tailed bats *Tadarida macrotis* (Gray) in Chihuahua, Mexico. *Amer. Midl. Nat.* 88:268–270.

_____. 1972*b*. Status of *Leptonycteris nivalis* (Phyllostomatidae) in Big Bend National Park, Texas. *Southw. Nat.* 17:287–292.

_____. 1973*a*. Big Bend National Park mammals field checklist. Big Bend Natural Hist. Assoc., Big Bend National Park.

_____. 1973*b*. Ecology of the 18 species of Chiroptera at Big Bend National Park, Texas. Parts 1 and 2. *Northw. Missouri State Univ. Studies,* Vol. 34.

_____. 1975. The red bat in Big Bend National Park, Texas. *Southw. Nat.* 20:418–419.

Easterla, David A., and J. Baccus. 1973. A collection of bats from the Fronteriza Mountains, Coahuila, Mexico. *Southw. Nat.* 17:423–428.

Easterla, David A., and P. Easterla. 1969. America's rarest mammal. *Nat. Wildl.* Aug.–Sept., pp. 15–18.

Easterla, David A., and J. O. Whitaker. 1972. Food habits of some bats from Big Bend National Park, Texas. *J. Mamm.* 53:887–890.

Findley, James S. and W. Caire. 1977. The status of mammals in the northern region of the Chihuahuan Desert. In *Trans. Sympos. Biol. Resources Chihuahuan Desert Region, U.S. and Mexico,* edited by Roland H. Wauer and David H. Riskind. USDI, National Park Service Trans. Proc. Ser. No. 3.

Forbes, Richard B. 1963. Some aspects of the life history of the silky pocket mouse. Typed report to National Park Service.

Hammerstrom, F. 1949. Checklist of mammals—Big Bend. Master's thesis, Sul Ross State College.

Jaeger, Edmund C. 1950. *Our desert neighbors*. Stanford: Stanford University Press.

Jennings, W. S., and J. T. Harris. 1953. *The collared peccary in Texas*. Austin: Texas Game and Fish Commission.

Judd, Frank W. 1967. Notes on some mammals from Big Bend National Park. *Southw. Nat.* 12:192–194.

Krausmann, Paul R. 1976. Ecology of Carmen Mountains white-tailed deer. Ph.D. dissertation, University of Idaho.

Kucera, Thomas A. 1976. Social behavior during rut and breeding season of the desert mule deer. Master's thesis, University of Michigan.

McBride, Roy T. 1977. The status and ecology of the mountain lion (*Felis concolor stanleyana*) of the Texas-Mexico border. Master's thesis, Sul Ross State University.

McDougall, W. B. 1935. The unique mammalian fauna of the proposed Big Bend International Park. Typed report to National Park Service.

Mearns, Edgar A. 1907. Mammals of the Mexican boundary of the United States, part I. *U.S. Nat. Mus. Bull.* 56.

Milstead, William M., and D. W. Tinkle. 1959. Notes on the porcupine (*Erithizon dorsatum*) in Texas. *Southw. Nat.* 3:236–237.

Rasp, Richard A. 1964. A population study of the yellow-nosed cotton rat in Big Bend National Park. Typed report to National Park Service.

Raun, Gerald G. 1962. A bibliography of the recent mammals of Texas. *Texas Mem. Mus. Bull.* 3.

Russell, R. J., and R. H. Baker. 1955. Geographic variation in the pocket gopher *Cratogeomys castanops* in Coahuila, Mexico. *Univ. Kansas Publ., Mus. Nat. Hist.* 7:593–608.

Schmidly, David J. 1977a. *The mammals of Trans-Pecos Texas*. College Station: Texas A&M University Press.

———. 1977b. Factors governing the distribution of mammals in the Chihuathe Chihuahuan Desert region. In *Trans. Sympos. Biol. Resources Chihuahuan Desert Region, U.S. and Mexico*, edited by Roland H. Wauer and David H. Riskind. USDI, National Park Service Trans. Proc. Ser. No. 3.

Scudday, James F. 1977a. *The vertebrate fauna of the Colorado Canyon area, Presidio County, Texas.* Austin: Texas Natural Areas Survey, University of Texas.

———. 1977b. *The vertebrate fauna of the Fresno–Chorro Canyon area, Presidio County, Texas.* Austin: Texas Natural Areas Survey, University of Texas.

———. 1977c. *The vertebrate fauna of the Solitario area, Brewster-Presidio Counties, Texas.* Austin: Texas Natural Areas Survey, University of Texas.

Smith, Donald D. 1975. Record of the red bat in Brewster County, Texas. *Texas J. Sci.* 26:601–602.

Stine, Walter D., Jr. 1975. Determination of winter-spring home ranges of coyotes *(Canis latrans)* by radio telemetry in Big Bend National Park, Texas. Master's thesis, Sul Ross State University.

Tamsitt, J. R. 1954. The mammals of two areas in the Big Bend region of Trans-Pecos Texas. *Texas J. Sci.* 6:33–61.

Taylor, Walter P., ed. 1956. *The deer of North America.* Harrisburg, Pa.: Stackpole Co.

Wallmo, O. C. 1959. Mountain lion records for Big Bend National Park, Texas. Typed report to National Park Service.

Walton, Don W., and J. D. Kimbrough. 1970. *Eumops perotis* from Black Gap Wildlife Refuge. *Southw. Nat.* 15:134–135.

Young, Stanley P., and E. A. Goldman. 1946. *The puma, mysterious American cat.* Washington, D.C.: American Wildlife Institute.

Birds

Allen, Therese M. 1977. A survey of the avifaunal associates of *Agave havardiana* Trel. in Big Bend National Park. Master's thesis, University of Texas, Arlington.

Allen, Therese M., and R. L. Neill. 1977. Avifaunal associates of *Agave havardiana* Trel. in Big Bend National Park. Typed report to National Park Service.

Bangs, Outram. 1925. The history and characters of *Vermivora crissalis* (Salvin and Godman) *Auk* 42:251–253.

Barlow, Jon C. 1967. Nesting of the black-capped vireo in the Chisos Mountains, Texas. *Condor* 69:605–606.

———. 1977. Effects of habitat attrition on Vireo distribution and population density in the northern Chihuahuan Desert. In *Trans. Sympos. Biol. Resources Chihuahuan Desert Region, U.S. and Mexico,* edited by Roland

H. Wauer and David H. Riskind. USDI, National Park Service Trans. Proc. Ser. No. 3.

Barlow, Jon C., and R. Johnson. 1967. Current status of the elf owl in the southwestern United States. *Southw. Nat.* 12:331–332.

Barlow, Jon C., and R. H. Wauer. 1971. The gray vireo *(Vireo vicinium)* Coues; Aves: Vireonidae wintering in the Big Bend region, west Texas. *Canadian J. Zool.* 49:953–955.

Beckham, C. W. 1888. Observations on the birds of southwestern Texas. *Proc. U.S. Nat. Mus.* 10:633–696.

Blake, Emmet R. 1949. The nest of the colima warbler in Texas. *Wilson Bull.* 61:65–67.

Borell, A. E. 1936. Birds observed in the Big Bend of Brewster County, Texas. Typed report to National Park Service.

———. 1938. New bird records for Brewster County, Texas. *Condor* 40:181–182.

Brandt, H. W. 1938. Two new birds from the Chisos Mountains, Texas. *Auk* 55:269–270.

———. 1940. *Texas bird adventures.* Cleveland: Bird Research Foundation.

Brodkorb, P. 1935. A new flycatcher from Texas. *Occas. Publ. Mus. Zool. Univ. Mich.* 306:1–3.

Brodrick, Harold J. 1960. Check-list of the birds of Big Bend National Park. Mimeographed.

Brown, D. E. 1977. Results of an attempt to determine the presence of Montezuma quail in the Chisos Mountains. Typed report to National Park Service.

Cottam, Clarence, and J. B. Trefethen, eds. 1968. *Whitewings—life history, status, and management of the white-winged dove.* Princeton, N.J.: D. Van Nostrand Co.

Cruickshank, Allen. 1950. Records from Brewster County, Texas. *Wilson Bull.* 62:217–219.

Cully, Jack F., Jr. 1972. Mobbing behavior of Mexican jays and scrub jays. Master's thesis, University of New Mexico.

Dixon, Keith L. 1955. An ecological analysis of the interbreeding of the crested titmice in Texas. *Univ. California Publ. Zool.* 54:125–206.

———. 1959. Ecological and distributional relations of desert scrub birds of western Texas. *Condor* 61:397–409.

Dixon, Keith L., and O. C. Wallmo. 1956. Some new bird records from Brewster County, Texas. *Condor* 58:166.

Easterla, David A. 1972. Specimens of black-throated blue warbler and yellow-green vireo from west Texas. *Condor* 74:489.

Easterla, David A., and R. H. Wauer. 1972. Bronzed cowbird in west Texas and two bill abnormalities. *Southw. Nat.* 17:293–295.

Hunt, W. Grainger. 1975. The Chihuahuan Desert peregrine falcon survey, 1975. Typed report to National Park Service.

————. 1976. Peregrine falcons in west Texas: results of the 1976 nesting survey. Mimeographed report to Texas Parks and Wildlife Department.

————. 1977. The significance of wilderness ecosystems in western Texas and adjacent regions in the ecology of the peregrine. In *Trans. Symp. Biol. Resources Chihuahuan Desert Region, U.S. and Mexico*, edited by Roland H. Wauer and David H. Riskind. USDI, National Park Service Trans. Proc. Ser. No. 3.

Johnson, Brenda S. 1976. Continuing studies of raptors in two national parks in western Texas, 1976. Typed report to National Park Service.

————. 1976. Peregrine falcons in west Texas: results of the 1976 nesting survey. Mimeographed report to Texas Parks and Wildlife Department.

Kowaleski, Charles T., and V. R. Wade. 1977. Texas peregrine eyrie search, 1977. Nesting peregrine falcons in Texas, 1977. Mimeographed report to National Park Service.

Kuban, Joe F., Jr. 1977. The ecological organization of hummingbirds in the Chisos Mountains, Big Bend National Park, Texas. Master's thesis, University of Texas, Arlington.

Ligon, J. David. 1968. The biology of the elf owl, *Micrathene whitneyi*. *Occas. Publ. Mus. Zool. Univ. Mich.* 136:1–70.

LoBello, Rick L. 1977. *Avifauna of the solitario with additional notes on the mammalian and herpetofauna, Brewster-Presidio Counties, Texas.* Austin: Texas Natural Areas Survey, University of Texas.

Marsh, Ernest G., Jr., and J. O. Stevenson. 1938. Bird records from northern Coahuila. *Auk* 55:286–287.

Marshall, Joe T. 1967. Parallel variation in north and middle American screech owls. Monographs of the West. Foun. Vert. Zool., Los Angeles, no. 1.

Miller, Alden H. 1954. Nomenclature of the black-throated sparrows of Chihuahua and western Texas. *Condor* 56:364–365.

———. 1955. The avifauna of the Sierra del Carmen of Coahuila, Mexico. *Condor* 57:154–178.

Montgomery, Thomas H., Jr. 1905. Summer resident birds of Brewster County, Texas. *Auk* 22:12–15.

Neill, Robert L., and T. M. Allen. 1977. Concentrated avian utilization of an early flowering century plant (*Agave havardiana*). Typed report to National Park Service.

Nelson, Richard Clay. 1970. An additional nesting record of the Lucifer hummingbird in the United States. *Southw. Nat.* 15:135–136.

Oberholser, Harry C. 1902. Some notes from western Texas. *Auk* 19:300–301.

Oberholser, Harry C., and E. B. Kincaid, Jr. 1974. *The bird life of Texas*. Austin: University of Texas Press.

Ohlendorf, Harry M., and R. F. Patton. 1971. Nesting record of Mexican duck (*Anas diazi*) in Texas. *Wilson Bull.* 83:97.

Palmer, Ralph S., ed. 1962. *Handbook of North American birds*. Vol. 1, *Loons through Flamingos*. New Haven: Yale University Press.

Peterson, Roger Tory. 1960. *A field guide to the birds of Texas*. Boston: Houghton Mifflin Co.

Peterson, Roger Tory, and E. L. Chalif. 1973. *A field guide to Mexican birds*. Boston: Houghton Mifflin Co.

Phillips, Allan R. 1977. Summary of avian resources of the Chihuahuan Desert region. In *Trans. Symp. Biol. Resources Chihuahuan Desert Region, U.S. and Mexico*, edited by Roland H. Wauer and David H. Riskind. USDI, National Park Service Trans. Proc. Ser. No. 3.

Phillips, Allan R.; J. Marshall; and G. Monson. 1964. *The birds of Arizona*. Tucson: University of Arizona Press.

Pulich, Warren M. 1963. Some recent records of the varied bunting (*Passerina versicolor*) for Texas. *Condor* 65:334–335.

Pulich, Warren M., and W. M. Pulich, Jr. 1963. The nesting of the Lucifer hummingbird in the United States. *Auk* 80:370–371.

Quillin, Roy W. 1935. New bird records from Texas. *Auk* 52:324–325.

Raitt, Ralph J. 1967. Relationships between black-eared and plain-eared forms of bushtits (*Psaltriparus*). *Auk* 84:503–528.

Raitt, Ralph J., and S. L. Pimm. 1977. Temporal changes in northern Chihuahuan Desert bird communities. In *Trans. Symp. Biol. Resources Chihuahuan Desert Region, U.S. and Mexico*, edited by Roland H. Wauer and David H. Riskind. USDI, National Park Service Trans. Proc. Ser. No. 3.

Robinson, Sharla M. 1973. Ethological study of *Vermivora crissalis* in the Chisos Mountains, Texas. Master's thesis, Sul Ross State University.

Scott, Peter E. 1977. Quarterly reports of bird observations in Big Bend National Park. Typed reports to National Park Service.

Snyder, Dorothy E. 1957. A recent Colima warbler's nest. *Auk* 74:97–98.

Sprunt, Alexander, Jr. 1950. The Colima warbler of the Big Bend. *Audubon Mag.* 52:84–90.

Stevenson, James O., and T. F. Smith. 1938. Additions to the Brewster County, Texas, bird list. *Condor* 40:184.

Strecker, John K., Jr. 1930. *Field notes on western Texas birds, pt.1. Contr. Baylor Univ. Mus.* no. 22.

Sutton, George Miksch. 1935. An expedition to the Big Bend Country. *The Cardinal* 4:1–7.

———. 1939. *Birds in the wilderness.* New York: Macmillan Co.

———. 1951. *Mexican birds: first impressions.* Norman: University of Oklahoma Press.

Sutton, George Miksch, and J. Van Tyne. 1935. A new red-tailed hawk from Texas. *Occas. Publs. Mus. Zool. Univ. Mich.* 321:1–6.

Thompson, William Lay. 1953. The ecological distribution of the birds of the Black Gap Area, Brewster County, Texas. *Texas J. Sci.* 5:158–177.

Van Tyne, Josselyn. 1929. Notes on some birds of the Chisos Mountains of Texas. *Auk* 46:204–206.

———. 1933. The 1932 Chisos Mountains expedition. *Rept. Dir. Univ. Mich. Mus. Zool.* 1931–1932:19–21.

———. 1936. The discovery of the nest of the Colima warbler (*Vermivora crissalis*). *Occas. Publ. Mus. Zool. Univ. Mich.* 33:5–11.

Van Tyne, Josselyn, and G. M. Sutton. 1937. The birds of Brewster County, Texas. *Occas. Publ. Mus. Zool. Univ. Mich.* 37:1–119.

Wallmo, O. C. 1956. Ecology of scaled quail in west Texas. Typed report to National Park Service.

Wauer, Roland H. 1967a. Checklist of birds of Big Bend National Park. Mimeographed.

———. 1967b. Colima warbler census in Big Bend's Chisos Mountains. *Nat. Parks Mag.* 41:8–10.

———. 1967c. First thick-billed kingbird record for Texas. *Southw. Nat.* 12:485–486.

————. 1967*d*. Further evidence of bushtit lumping in Texas. *Bull. Texas Ornith. Soc.* 1(5–6):1.

————. 1967*e*. Report on the Colima warbler census. Mimeographed.

————. 1967*f*. Winter and early spring birds in Big Bend. *Bull. Texas Ornith. Soc.* 1:7–14.

————. 1968. The groove-billed ani in Texas. *Southw. Nat.* 13:452.

————. 1969*a*. Hummingbirds of Big Bend. *Bull. Texas Ornith. Soc.* 3:18.

————. 1969*b*. Report on the 1969 Colima warbler census. Typed report to National Park Service.

————. 1969*c*. Winter bird records from the Chisos Mountains and vicinity. *Southw. Nat.* 14:252–254.

————. 1970*a*. The occurrence of the black-vented oriole, *Icterus wagleri*, in the United States. *Auk* 87:811–812.

————. 1970*b*. Report of the 1970 Colima warbler census. Typed report to National Park Service.

————. 1970*c*. A second swallow-tailed kite record for Trans-Pecos Texas. *Wilson Bull.* 82:462.

————. 1970*d*. Upland plover at Big Bend National Park. *Southw. Nat.* 14:361–362.

————. 1971*a*. Big Bend National Park. In *Birder's guide to the Rio Grande Valley of Texas,* edited by James Lane, pp. 33–36. Sacramento: L & P Photo.

————. 1971*b*. Ecological distribution of birds of the Chisos Mountains, Texas. *Southw. Nat.* 16:1–29.

————. 1973*a*. *Birds of Big Bend National Park and vicinity*. Austin: University of Texas Press.

————. 1973*b*. Status of certain parulids in west Texas. *Southw. Nat.* 18:105–110.

————. 1973*c*. Bronzed cowbird extends range into the Texas Big Bend country. *Wilson Bull.* 85:343–344.

————. 1973*d*. Report on harlequin quail release. Typed report to National Park Service.

————. 1973*e*. *Naturalist's Big Bend*. Santa Fe, N. Mex.: Peregrine Prod.

————. 1977*a*. Changes in the breeding avifauna within the Chisos Mountains system. In *Trans. Symp. Biol. Resources Chihuahuan Desert Region, U.S.*

and Mexico, edited by Roland H. Wauer and David H. Riskind. USDI, National Park Service Trans. Proc. Ser. No. 3.

———. 1977*b*. Significance of the west Texas Rio Grande upon avifauna within riparian systems throughout the southwestern U.S. *Proc. Symp.: Importance, preservation, and management of riparian habitat: a symposium.* USDA, Forest Service, Gen. Tech. Report RM-43.

———. 1977*c*. Interrelations between a Harris' hawk and a badger. *Western Birds* 8:155.

———. 1979. Colima warbler status at Big Bend National Park, Texas. *Proc. First Conf. Sci. Res. in National Parks, November 1976,* edited by Robert M. Linn. USDI, National Park Service Trans. Proc. Ser. No. 5.

———. In press. The birds of the Lower Canyons of the Rio Grande. In *Lower Canyons of the Rio Grande.* Austin: Texas Natural Area Survey.

Wauer, Roland H., and D. G. Davis. 1972. Cave swallows in Big Bend National Park, Texas. *Condor* 74:482.

Wauer, Roland H., and J. D. Ligon. 1977. Distributional relations of breeding avifauna of four southwest mountain ranges. In *Trans. Symp. Biol. Resources Chihuahuan Desert Region, U.S. and Mexico,* edited by Roland H. Wauer and David H. Riskind. USDI, National Park Service Trans. Proc. Ser. No. 3.

Wauer, Roland H., and M. K. Rylander. 1968. Anna's hummingbird in west Texas. *Auk* 85:501.

Wauer, Roland H., and J. Scudday. 1972. Occurrence and status of certain Charadriiformes in the Texas Big Bend country. *Southw. Nat.* 17:210–211.

Webster, J. Dan. 1977. The avifauna of the southern part of the Chihuahuan Desert. In *Trans. Sympos. Biol. Resources Chihuahuan Desert region, U.S. and Mexico,* edited by Roland H. Wauer and David H. Riskind. USDI, National Park Service Trans. Proc. Ser. No. 3.

Whitson, Martha Anne. 1971. Field and laboratory investigations of the ethology of courtship and copulation in the greater roadrunner. Ph.D. dissertation, University of Oklahoma.

———. 1976. Courtship behavior of the greater roadrunner. *Living Bird,* June, pp. 215–256.

Reptiles and Amphibians

Brown, Bryce C. 1950. *Annotated check list of the reptiles and amphibians of Texas.* Baylor University Studies. Waco: Baylor University Press.

Brown, Teddy L. 1970. Ecological distribution of spiny lizards (*Scelophorus*) in Big Bend National Park, Texas. Master's thesis, University of New Mexico.

Conant, Roger. 1969. A review of the water snakes of the genus *Natrix* in Mexico. *Bull. Amer. Mus. Nat. Hist.* 142:1–140.

———. 1975. *A field guide to reptiles and amphibians of eastern North America*. Boston: Houghton Mifflin Co.

———. 1977. Semiaquatic reptiles and amphibians of the Chihuahuan Desert and their relationships to drainage patterns of the region. In *Trans. Sympos. Biol. Resources Chihuahuan Desert Region, U.S. and Mexico*, edited by Roland H. Wauer and David H. Riskind. USDI, National Park Service Trans. Proc. Ser. No. 3.

Degenhardt, William G. 1966. A method of counting some diurnal ground lizards of the genera *Holbrookia* and *Cnemidorphorus* with results from the Big Bend National Park. *Amer. Midl. Nat.* 75:61–100.

———. 1969. A report on the current status of the Big Bend National Park herpetofauna. Typed report to National Park Service.

———. 1970. Population status of diurnal lizards. Mimeographed.

Degenhardt, William G.; T. L. Brown; and D. A. Easterla. 1975. The taxonomic status of *Tantilla cucullata* and *Tantilla diabola*. *Texas J. Sci.* 27:225–234.

Easterla, David A. 1975a. *An annotated checklist of the amphibians and reptiles of Big Bend National Park, Texas*. Big Bend Nat. Hist. Assoc.

———. 1975b. Reproductive and ecological observations of *Tantilla rubra cucullata* from Big Bend National Park, Texas (*Serpentes:* Colubridae). *Herpet.* 31:234–236.

Easterla, David A., and R. C. Reynolds. 1975. Additional records and ecological notes on the reticulated gecko, *Coleonyx reticulatus* (Davis and Dixon), from the southern Trans-Pecos of southwestern Texas. *J. Herp.* 9:233–236.

Gehlbach, Frederick R., and J. K. Baker. 1962. Kingsnakes allied with *Lampropeltis mexicana*: taxonomy and natural history. *Copeia* 1962:291–300.

Gehlbach, Frederick R., and C. J. McCoy, Jr. 1965. Additional observations on variation and distribution of the gray-banded kingsnakes, *Lampropeltis mexicana* (Garman). *Herpet.* 21:35–38.

Gloyd, Howard K., and R. Conant. 1943. A synopsis of the American forms of *Agkistrodon* (Copperheads and moccasins). *Bull. Chi. Acad. Sci.*, 7:147–170.

Hamilton, Rodgers D. 1947. The range of *Pseudemys scripta Gaigeae. Copeia* 1947:65–66.

Jacob, James S. 1977. An evaluation of the possibility of hybridization between the rattlesnakes *Crotalus atrox* and *C. sculutalus* in the southwestern United States. *Southw. Nat.* 22:469–485.

Jameson, D. L., and A. G. Flury. 1949. The reptiles and amphibians of the Sierra Viejo. *Texas J. Sci.* 1:54–79.

Kauffeld, Carl F. 1960. The search for *subocularis. Phil. Herp. Soc.* 8, 3:9–15.

———. 1969. *Snakes, the keeper and the kept.* New York: Doubleday Co.

Legler, John M. 1960. Remarks on the natural history of the Big Bend slider, *Pseudemys scripta Gaigeae* Hartweg. *Herpet.* 16:139–140.

Loomis, Richard B., and F. C. Jahn. 1973. Notes on one juvenile and two adult *Coleonyx reticularis,* and their ecoparasitic mites. Typed report to National Park Service.

Lucchino, Ronald V. 1970. Distribution of two lizards, *Cnemidophorus tigris* and *C. scalaris,* in Pine Canyon, Big Bend National Park, Texas. Master's thesis, University of New Mexico.

McCoy, Clarence J., Jr. 1961. Additional records of *Ficimia cana* from Mexico and Texas. *Herpet.* 17:215.

McCoy, Clarence J., Jr., and F. R. Gehlbach. 1968. Cloacal hemorrhage and the defense display of the Colubrid snakes. *Texas Acad. Sci.* 19:349–353.

Milstead, William W. 1953*a*. Ecological distribution of the lizards of the La Mota Mountain region of Trans-Pecos Texas. *Texas J. Sci.* 4:403–415.

———. 1953*b*. Geographic variation in the garter snake, *Thamnophis crytopsis. Texas J. Sci.* 5:348–379.

———. 1957. Some aspects of competition in natural populations of whiptail lizards (Genus *Cnemidophorus*). *Texas J. Sci.* 9:410–447.

———. 1959. Drift-fence trapping of lizards on the Black Gap Wildlife Management Area of southwestern Texas. *Texas J. Sci.* 11:150–157.

———. 1961. Competitive relations in lizard populations. In *Vertebrate Speciation,* edited by W. F. Blair, pp. 460–489. Austin: University of Texas Press.

———. 1965. Changes in competing populations of whiptail lizards (*Cnemidophorus*) in southwestern Texas. *Amer. Midl. Nat.* 73:75–80.

———. 1969. Studies of the evolution of box turtles (Genus *Terrapene*). *Bull. Florida State Mus.* 14:1–113.

_____. 1970a. Late summer behavior of the lizards *Sceloporus merriamii* and *Urosaurus ornatus* in the field. *Herpet.* 26:343–354.

_____. 1970b. On the problems of home range measurements and individual recognition in lizard ecological studies. *Herpet.* 26:3–17.

_____. 1971. Stomach analysis of the crevice spiny lizard (*Sceloporus poinsetti*). *Herpet.* 27:147–149.

_____. 1977. The Black Gap whiptail lizards after twenty years. In *Trans. Sympos. Biol. Resources Chihuahuan Desert Region, U.S. and Mexico,* edited by Roland H. Wauer and David H. Riskind. USDI, National Park Service Trans. Proc. Ser. No. 3.

Minton, Sherman A., Jr. 1959. Observations on amphibians and reptiles of the Big Bend region of Texas. *Southw. Nat.* 3:28–54.

Morafka, David S. 1977. Is there a Chihuahuan Desert? A quantitative evaluation through a herpetofaunal perspective. In *Trans. Sympos. Biol. Resources Chihuahuan Desert Region, U.S. and Mexico,* edited by Roland H. Wauer and David H. Riskind. USDI, National Park Service Trans. Proc. Ser. No. 3.

Murray, Leo T. 1939. Annotated list of amphibians and reptiles from the Chisos Mountains. *Contr. Baylor Univ. Mus.* 24:1–16.

Peters, James A. 1951. Studies of the lizards *Holbrookia texana* (Troschel) with distributions of two new subspecies. *Occas. Publ. Mus. Zool. Univ. Mich.* 537.

Priest, Joe W. 1972. Morphological and behavioral evidence as to the taxonomic status of two subspecies of *Sceloporus merriami*. Master's thesis, Sul Ross State University.

Punzo, Fred. 1974. An analysis of the stomach contents of the gecko, *Coleonyx brevis*. *Copeia* 1974: 779–780.

Raun, Gerald G., and F. R. Gehlbach. 1972. Amphibians and reptiles in Texas. *Dallas Mus. Nat. Hist. Bull.* 2.

Schmidt, Karl P. 1925. Notes on *Elaphe subocularis* (Brown). *Copeia* 1925 (1):87–88.

_____. 1940. Notes on Texas snakes of the genus *Salvadora*. Field Mus. Nat. Hist. Zool. Ser. 24:163–150.

Schmidt, Karl P., and T. F. Smith. 1944. Amphibians and reptiles of the Big Bend region of Texas. Field Mus. Nat. Hist. Zool. Ser. 29:75–96.

Schmidt, Karl P., and D. W. Owens. 1944. Amphibians and reptiles of northern Coahuila, Mexico. Field Mus. Nat. Hist. Zool. Ser. 29:97–115.

Scudday, James F. 1977. Some recent changes in the herpetofauna of the northern Chihuahuan Desert. In *Trans. Sympos. Biol. Resources Chihuahuan Desert Region, U.S. and Mexico*, edited by Roland H. Wauer and David H. Riskind. USDI, National Park Service Trans. Proc. Ser. No. 3.

Seifert, W., and R. W. Murphy. 1972. Additional specimens of *Coleonyx reticulatus* (Davis and Dixon) from the Black Gap Wildlife Management Area, Texas. *Herpet.* 28:24–26.

Seifert, W.; F. Rainwater; and T. Kasper. 1973. Significant range extensions with field and lab notes for the reticulated gecko, *Coleonyx reticulatus* (Davis and Dixon). *Southw. Nat.* 18:101–103.

Smith, Hobart M., and O. Sanders. 1952. Distributional data on Texas amphibians and reptiles. *Texas J. Sci.* 2:204–219.

Smith, Hobart M., and J. E. Werler. 1970. The status of the northern red black-headed snake *(Tantilla diabola)* Fouquette and Potter. *J. Herp.* 3:172–173.

Smith, Tarleton F. 1936. Narrative report: herpetology. Typed report to National Park Service.

Stebbins, Robert C. 1966. *A field guide to western reptiles and amphibians.* Boston: Houghton Mifflin Co.

Strecker, John D., Jr. 1909. Reptiles and amphibians collected in Brewster County, Texas. *Baylor Univ. Bull.* 12:11–15.

Treadwell, R. W. 1966. Distribution of the leopard lizard, *Crotaphytus wislizeni*, in Texas. *Southw. Nat.* 11:412.

Wauer, Roland H., and G. Burdick. 1974. Range extension of Mediterranean gecko in Coahuila, Mexico. *Southw. Nat.* 19:446.

Fish

Campbell, Lawrence S. 1962. Basic survey and inventory of species, as well as their distribution in the Rio Grande River of Texas in region 3-B. Fed. Aid Proj. F-5-R-8. Texas Game and Fish Commission.

Contreras-Balderas, Salvador. 1977. Speciation aspects and man-made community composition changes in Chihuahuan Desert Fishes. In *Trans. Sympos. Biol. Resources Chihuahuan Desert Region, U.S. and Mexico*, edited by Roland H. Wauer and David H. Riskind. USDI, National Park Service Trans. Proc. Ser. No. 3.

Hubbs, Carl L. 1940. Fishes from the Big Bend region of Texas. *Trans. Texas Acad. Sci.* 23:3–12.

Hubbs, Clark. 1954. Corrected distribution records of Texas fresh water fishes. *Texas J. Sci.* 6:277–291.

_____. 1956. Key to the fresh water fishes of Texas. Mimeographed.

Hubbs, Clark, and H. J. Brodrick. 1963. Current abundance of *Gambusia gaigei*, an endangered fish species. *Southw. Nat.* 8:46–48.

Hubbs, Clark, and R. H. Wauer. 1972. Seasonal changes in the fish fauna of Tornillo Creek, Brewster County, Texas. *Southw. Nat.* 17:375–379.

Hubbs, Clark; J. Johnson; and R. H. Wauer. 1977. Habitat management plan, Big Bend Gambusia, Big Bend National Park. Typed report to National Park Service.

Hubbs, Clark, et al. 1977. Fishes inhabiting the Rio Grande, Texas and Mexico, between El Paso and Pecos confluence. *Importance, preservation, and management of riparian habitat: a symposium.* USDA, Forest Service, Gen. Tech. Report RM-43.

Miller, Robert Rush. 1961. Man and the changing fish fauna of the American Southwest. *Papers Mich. Acad. Sci. Arts. Letters.* 46:365–404.

_____. 1963. Preliminary list of rare, restricted, and/or threatened North American fresh water fishes. Mimeographed.

_____. 1977. Composition and derivation of the native fish fauna of the Chihuahuan Desert region. In *Trans. Sympos. Biol. Resources Chihuahuan Desert Region, U.S. and Mexico,* edited by Roland H. Wauer and David H. Riskind. USDI, National Park Service Trans. Proc. Ser. No. 3.

Invertebrates

Arnett, Ross H., Jr. 1965. Species of Oedemeridae of the Big Bend region of Texas. *Proc. U.S. Nat. Mus.* 118:47–56.

Baker, R. H. 1938. Preliminary investigation of the insects of the proposed Big Bend National Park, Brewster County, Texas. Typed report to National Park Service.

Berry, Richard Lee. 1974. New species of *Cryptadius* from Texas and Sonora (Coleoptera: Tenebrionidae). *Proc. Entom. Soc. Wash.* 76:172–177.

Blanchard, Andre. 1966. A new species of *Glaucina* (Geometridae) from Texas. *J. Lepid. Soc.* 20:133–145.

_____. 1968. New moths from Texas (Noctuidae, Tortricidae). *J. Lepid. Soc.* 22.

_____. 1970. Observations of some Phycitinae (Phyralidae) of Texas with descriptions of two new species. *J. Lepid. Soc.* 24:249–255.

_____. 1971a. A new species in the genus *Ursia* Barnes and McDonnough (Lepidoptera: Notoontidae). *Proc. Ent. Soc. Wash.* 73:303–305.

_____. 1971b. Notes on three species of *Heterocampa doubleday* with description of a new species (Lepidoptera: Notodontidae). *Proc. Entom. Soc. Wash.* 73:249–254.

_____. 1972. More new moths from Texas (Noctuidae). *J. Lepid. Soc.* 26:56–63.

_____. 1973. Record and illustration of some interesting moths flying in Texas (Aphingidae, Ctenuchidae, Noctuidae, Notodontidae, Geometridae, Phralidae, Cossidae). *J. Lepid. Soc.* 27:103–109.

Burns, John M., and R. O. Kendall. 1969. Ecologic and spatial distribution of *Pyrgus oileus* and *Pyrgus philetas* (Lepidoptera: Hesperiidae), at their northern distributional limits. *Psyche* 76:41–53.

Cheatum, E. P., and R. W. Fullington. 1971a. The recent and Pleistocene members of the Gastropod family Polygryridae in Texas. *The aquatic and land Mollusca of Texas*, part 1. *Dallas Mus. Nat. Hist. Bull.* 1.

_____. 1971b. Keys to the families of the recent land and freshwater snails of Texas. *The aquatic and land Mollusca of Texas*, supplement. *Dallas Mus. Nat. Hist. Bull.* 1.

_____. 1973. The recent and Pleistocene members of the Pupillidae and Urocoptidae (Gastropoda) in Texas. *The aquatic and land Mollusca of Texas*, part 2. *Dallas Mus. Nat. Hist. Bull.* 1.

Cheatum, Elmer P.; R. W. Fullington; and W. L. Pratt, Jr. 1972. Molluscan records from west Texas. *Sterkiana* 46:6–10.

Clench, Harry K. 1963. Butterflies (*Rhopalocera*) known from Big Bend National Park. Typed report to National Park Service.

Cohn, Theodore J. 1965. The arid-land Katydids of the North American genus *Neobarraita* (Orthoptera: Tettigonlidae), their systematics and a reconstruction of their history. *Occas. Publ. Mus. Zool. Univ. Mich.* 126.

Crawford, C. S. 1974. The role of *Orthoporus ornatus* millipedes in a desert ecosystem. U.S. International Biological Program Research Memo 74-34.

David, Donald R. 1967. A revision of the moths of the subfamily Proxinae. *Smithsonian Inst. Bull.* 222.

Easterla, David A. 1975. Giant desert centipede preys upon snake. *Southw. Nat.* 20:411.

Freeman, H. A. 1952. Two new species of *Megathymus* from Texas and Mexico (Lepidoptera, Rhopalocera, Megathymidae). *Amer. Mus. Novitates* 1593:1–9.

————. 1955. Four new species of *Megathymus* (Lepidoptera, Rhopalocera, Megathymidae). *Amer. Mus. Novitates*, 1711:1–20.

Fullington, R. W., and W. L. Pratt, Jr. 1974. The Helicinidae, Carychiidae, Achatinidae, Bradybaenidae, Balimulidae, Cionellidae, Haplotrematidae, Helicidae, Oreohelicidae, Spiraxidae, Streptaxidae, Strabilopsidae, Thysanophoridae, Valloniidae, (Gastropoda) in Texas. *The aquatic and land Mollusca of Texas*, part 3. *Dallas Mus. Nat. Hist. Bull.* 1.

Gertsch, W. J. 1939. Report on a collection of Arachnida from the Chisos Mountains. *Contr. Baylor Univ. Mus.* 24:17–26.

Gertsch, W. J., and M. Soleglad. 1972. Studies of North American scorpions of the genera *Uroctonus* and *Vejovis* (Scorpionida, Vejovidae). *Bull. Amer. Mus. Nat. Hist.* 148, 4:549–608.

Gloyd, Lenora K. 1958. The dragonfly fauna of the Big Bend region of Trans-Pecos Texas. *Occas. Publ. Mus. Zool. Univ. Mich.* 593:1–23.

Howden, Henry F. 1960*a*. A new species of *Phyllophaga* from the Big Bend region of Texas and Coahuila, with notes on other *Scarabaedae* of the area. *Canadian Entom.* 92:457–464.

————. 1960*b*. Two new species of *Cytrinus Leconte* (Coleoptera: Cerambycidae). *Canadian Entom.* 92:173–177.

Jones, H. J., and W. W. Wirth. 1958. New records, synonyms, and species of Texas Culicoides (Diptera, Heleidae). *J. Kan. Entom. Soc.* 31:81–91.

Kendall, Roy O. 1971. The butterflies and skippers of Texas. Typed report to National Park Service.

————. 1972. Three butterfly species (Lycaenidae, Nymphalidae, and Heliconiidae) new to Texas and the United States. *J. Lepid. Soc.* 26:49–56.

————. 1976. Larval foodplants and life history notes for eight moths from Texas and Mexico. *J. Lepid. Soc.* 30:264–271.

Kinsey, A. C. 1935. Notes of faunal relations of Cynipidae (Gall Wasps). Typed report to National Park Service.

Knull, Joseph N. 1960. A new subspecies of *Agrilias* from Texas (Coleoptera: Buprestidae).*Ohio J. Sci.* 60:321.

Krombein, Karl C., and B. D. Burks. 1967. *Hymenoptera of American north of Mexico.* USDA Monograph no. 2.

Loomis, Richard B. 1971. The genus *Euschoengastoides* (Acarina: Trombiculidae) from North America. *J. Parasit.* 57:689–707.

Loomis, Richard B., and D. A. Crossley, Jr. 1963. New species and new records of chiggers (Acarina) from Texas. *Acarologia* 5:371–383.

Loomis, Richard B., J. T. Baccus; and W. J. Wrenn. 1972. The chiggers (Acarina: Trombicilidae) of Big Bend National Park, Texas. Typed report to National Park Service.

Loomis, Richard B., and W. J. Wrenn. No date. Additional chiggers (Acarina: Trombiculidae) from vertebrate hosts of Big Bend National Park and vicinity, Brewster County, Texas. Typed report to National Park Service.

McElvare, Rowland R. 1950. A new Grotella from southwest Texas (Lepidoptera, Phalaenidae). *Bull. Brooklyn Ent. Soc.* 45:117–118.

——. 1966. New *Heliothid* moth from the southwestern United States (Noctuidae). *J. Lepid. Soc.* 20:91–94.

Milstead, William W. 1958. A list of Arthropods found in the stomachs of whiptail lizards from stations in southwestern Texas. *Texas J. Sci.* 10:443–446.

O'Brien, Charles W. 1973. *Rhianisus chisosensis*, a new species of Cossonine weevil in a genus new to the United States (Coleoptera: Curulionidae). *The Coleopt. Bull.* 27:7–9.

Pratt, W. L. 1971. *Humboltiana agavophile*, a new Helmanthoglyptid land snail from the Chisos Mountains, Big Bend National Park, Texas. *Southw. Nat.* 15:429–435.

——. 1972*a*. Ecological distribution and zoogeography of the land snails of the Chisos Mountains, Big Bend National Park, Texas. Master's thesis, University of Texas, Arlington.

——. 1972*b*. Land snails of the Chisos Mountains, Big Bend National Park, Texas. *Bull. Am. Malacol. Union, Inc.* 1971:8–9.

Riddle, Wayne A. 1975. Water relations and humidity-related metabolism of the desert snail *Rabdotus schiedeanus* (Pfeifer) (Bulimulidae). *Comp. Biochem. Physiol.* 51A:579–583.

——. 1977. Comparative respiratory physiology of a desert snail *Rabdotus schiedeanus*, and a garden snail, *Helix aspersa. Comp. Biochem. Physiol.* 56A:369–373.

Sabath, Laura Elsa. 1967. Report on Arachnid and Myriapod collection. Typed report to National Park Service.

Sanderson, Milton W. 1939. A new genus of Scarabaedae with descriptions and notes on Phyllophaga. *J. Kansas Entom. Soc.* 12:1–15.

Scullen, H. A. 1948. New species in the genus *Eucerceris* with notes on recorded species and a revised key to the genus. *Pan-Pacif. Entom.* 14:155–164.

———. 1968. A revision of the genus *Eucerceris Cresson* (Hymenoptera: Sphecidae). *Smithsonian Inst. Bull.* 268.

Scullen, H. A., and J. L. World. 1969. Biology of wasps of the tribe Cererini, with a list of Coleoptera used as prey. *Annals Entom. Soc. Amer.* 62:209–214.

Smith, Bruce B. 1972. Representative of the class Arachnida specific to the Big Bend area. Typed report, Westminister Coll.

Stahnke, Herbert L. 1956. A new species of scorpion of the Buthidae: *Centruroides pantheriensis*. *Entom. News* 67:15–19.

———. 1967. *Diplocentrus bigbendsis*, a new species of scorpion. *Entom. News* 78:173–179.

Stehr, Frederick W., and E. F. Cook. 1968. A revision of the genus *Malacosoma* Hubner North American (Lepidoptera: Lasiocampidae): systematics, biology, immatures, and parasites. *Smithsonian Inst. Bull.* 276.

Tinkham, Ernest R. 1941. Biological and faunistic notes on the Cicadidae of the Big Bend region of Trans-Pecos Texas. *J. New York Entom. Soc.* 49:165–183.

———. 1943. Description and biological notes on a new Saturnid of the genus *Pseudohazis* from the Big Bend region of Texas. *Canadian Entom.* 75:159–162.

———. 1944. Faunistic notes on the diurnal Lepidoptera of the Big Bend region of Trans-Pecos Texas, with description of a new Melitaea. *Canadian Entom.* 76:11–18.

———. 1948. Faunistic and ecological studies on the Orthoptera of the Big Bend region of Trans-Pecos Texas, with especial reference to the Orthopteras zones and faunae of midwestern North America. *Amer. Midl. Nat.* 40:521–663.

Triplehorn, Charles A. 1963. A synopsis of the genus *Cryptoglossa Solier* (Coleoptera: Tenebrionidae). *Coleop. Bull.* 18:43–52.

———. 1967. Notes on the species of *Megasida* Casey from the United States (Coleoptera: Tenebrionidae). *Ohio J. Sci.* 76:38–41.

———. 1968. Generic classification in *Coniotini* and description of new species of *Eusattus* from Texas. *Entom. Soc. Amer.* 61:376–380.

_____. 1971. A new species of *Eleodes* from Texas with notes on the subgenus *Promus* (Coleoptera: Tenebrionidae). *Ohio J. Sci.* 71:56–59.

Van Pelt, Arnold. 1971. Trophobiosis and feeding habitats of *Liemetopum apiculatum* (Hymenoptera: Formicidae) in the Chisos Mountains, Texas. *Annals Entom. Soc. Amer.* 64:1186.

_____. 1975. Ants collected from the Chisos Mountains in Big Bend National Park. Typed report to National Park Service.

Van Pelt, Arnold, and S. A. Van Pelt. 1972. *Microdon* (Diptera: Syrphidae) in nests of *Monomorium* (Hymenoptera: Formicidae) in Texas. *Annals Entom. Soc. Amer.* 65:977–978.

Werner, Floyd G. 1974. A new genus of primitive Meloidae from west Texas (Coleoptera). *Psyche* 81:147–154.

Wirth, Willis W., and R. H. Jones. 1957. The North American subspecies of *Culicoides variipennis*. *USDA Bull.* 1170:1–35.